248.8   Baxter, Anne
B   Woman's work

DATE DUE			
FEB. 2 3 1997			

A Guide to Growth and Self-Discovery

WOMAN'S WORK

Edited by

Anne Baxter &
Nora O. Lozano-Díaz

HERALD PRESS
Scottdale, Pennsylvania
Waterloo, Ontario

Library of Congress Cataloging-in-Publication Data
Woman's work : a guide to growth and self-discovery / edited by
    Anne Baxter and Nora O. Lozano-Díaz.
        p. cm.
    Includes bibliographical references.
    ISBN 0-8361-3695-0
        1. Women—Religious life. 2. Woman (Christian theology)
    I. Lozano-Díaz, Nora O., 1962- II. Baxter, Anne, 1964-
    BV4527.W596 1994
    248.8'43—dc20   94-34353
                                                          CIP

The paper used in this publication is recycled and meets the mini-
mum requirements of American National Standard for Information
Sciences— Permanence of Paper for Printed Library Materials, ANSI
Z39.48-1984.

WOMAN'S WORK
Copyright © 1994 by Herald Press, Scottdale, Pa. 15683
        Published simultaneously in Canada by Herald Press,
        Waterloo, Ont. N2L 6H7. All rights reserved
Library of Congress Catalog Number: 94-34353
International Standard Book Number: 0-8361-3695-0
Printed in the United States of America
Cover and book design by Paula M. Johnson

1 2 3 4 5 6 7 8 9 10 00 99 98 97 96 95 94

To all the important women in our lives:
they have embodied for us the richness of
the past, the struggles of the present,
and the hope of tomorrow.

Contents

Preface

*T*his book was born out of frustration. Hungry to know more about the different issues that affect women's lives, we found our wish frustrated by the busy pace of our days and the lack of time to delve deeply into the issues. Being full-time seminary students, we had little time and energy left to work on personal growth that would help us develop a stronger sense of self.

During our second and third year of graduate studies, we became members of a support group for women seminarians. The group discussed two books—*Becoming Woman*, by Penelope Washbourn, and *The Dance of Anger*, by Harriet Goldhor Lerner. Although the two books were extremely helpful, at the group's conclusion we found ourselves hungry for more. We needed to cover more territory in less time. Many other issues had yet to be explored.

Through conversations with other Christian women, we found out that many of them were like us, eager to know more about issues facing women, but too busy with school, work, church, or family to read an entire book on each issue.

We began to see a need for a book written for occupied and searching Christian women which would offer material about women's issues in a brief but profound way. This book attempts to address that need.

Written in a personal and forthright way, this material gives a quick overview of the most pressing issues facing Christian women today. Each chapter provides introductory information on the topic, the main issues or questions relating to each topic, a series of reflection questions allowing each woman to wrestle personally with the topic, and a list of resources for further exploration.

The first chapter, "Women and Their Gifts," stresses the importance of knowing who we are and what unique gifts lie within us as daughters of God called to become co-creators with God. The chapters entitled "Women and Christ," "Women and the Image of God," and "Women and Spirituality" provide the Christian woman with a more wholistic perspective of God, Christ, and herself. These chapters also challenge the way women perceive themselves and their roles in the family, church, and society.

The piece on "Women and Their Learning Styles" encourages women to recognize, trust, and express their own inner voice. The material on "Women and Their Families" invites readers to understand and accept themselves better by going back and examining their families of origin. "Women and Their Self-Esteem" and "Women and Their Body Image" provide information about how to cope with and overcome issues of low self-esteem. The chapter on "Women and Their Sexuality" encourages women to see sexuality as a gift from God and as an integral part of themselves.

"Women and Intimacy," "Women and Their Anger," and "Women and Their Friendship" empower women to have healthier and more fulfilling relationships. The last section, "Women and Their Self-Care," encourages women to take care of themselves, explores why this is so hard to do, and reveals how it can be a rewarding discipline for women.

The decision to include these particular topics came out of our own journeys as Christian women and through our struggle to strengthen our relationships with God, ourselves, and each other. Our hope is that after working with this book, each woman will have a panoramic view of the issues affecting women's lives and a focused view of the ways these issues touch her personally.

The best way to use this book is in a support group setting where confidentiality, trust, love, and sisterhood are enhanced. A suggested size for this group is six to eight members, including the leaders. Our experience suggests that if each woman reads the material and works with the reflection questions in advance, two-hour meetings allow time for meaty discussions.

If you decide to use this book by yourself, leave some time for meditation between the reading of each chapter. Also, do not fall in the temptation of overlooking the reflection questions. They are designed to help you wrestle with the issues, so dig into them with gusto!

Finally we want to express our great appreciation to Carol, Helen, and Elouise for believing in this project and supporting it through their insightful and challenging writing; to Heather, Gretchen, Bunnie, Tracy, Mary, and Natalie—members of the first support group who tested this material—for their willingness to experiment with each one of these topics in a personal, committed, and courageous way; and to the Women's Concerns department of Eastern Baptist Theological Seminary, for their constant support and encouragement throughout this project.

—*Nora O. Lozano-Díaz, Vincentown, New Jersey*
—*Anne Baxter, Makuti, The Philippines*

WOMAN'S WORK

1

Women and Their Gifts

Anne Baxter

We cannot fool ourselves for long about what we are to do. Somewhere deep down in us is stored the secret, and when we are digging in the wrong place, we know it. The secret wants to be discovered and will not let us go in peace a way that is not ours.

Elizabeth O'Connor

I have two dwarf rabbits. I adopted them during my years at seminary. Kalah is small and black. When she first arrived, she was nervous and timid. When I approached, her eyes would bulge and her body would vibrate with fear. She came in a cage with Hazel, who is large and gray and quite fearless as far as rabbits go. Shortly after their arrival, Hazel began to pull out Kalah's hair to make a nest, which did little to improve Kalah's disposition. In somewhat of a quandary, I separated the rabbits, leaving Hazel in the cage and setting up a small box for Kalah in my bathroom.

While there was no lid on the box, Kalah was used to being caged, and she stayed in the box on her own accord for weeks. One day, however, I noticed that she had jumped out and was sitting on my bathroom floor. When I approached, she jumped back in. Now rabbits are like cats when it comes to little boxes, so I just let her be.

In a few weeks Kalah was roaming farther and farther in her new bathroom kingdom. She'd scamper up to sniff my toes when I was brushing my teeth and would haughtily push my hand away with her nose if I tried to pet her. She didn't venture beyond the bathroom door, however. At least not for a while. . . .

One day I came home to see Kalah sitting in the hallway staring at me with bright eyes. I shooed her into the bathroom and wondered how far she would roam. A few mornings later I was lying in bed half-awake when I felt a strange sensation at my feet. Kalah had jumped onto my bed.

From that time on, my room was Kalah's domain. She dug a hollow in the base of my fig tree, sat in the fireplace, crawled over my feet in the morning and sometimes, if I lay very still, would hop on up to sniff my face.

Kalah's black shape darting across the floor tickled me. Confined to a cage with Hazel she'd been a nervous, timid creature. Removed from Hazel and able to explore, her zest, curiosity, and independence emerged. She became a wild thing who jumped and poked and created a home for herself with what seemed almost humanlike intelligence and curiosity. She was becoming a rabbit, as she was created to be. I could see that in her own rabbit's way, she sensed that life was good.

Since Kalah's transformation, I often wonder what it must feel like to be fully alive as a woman. If I could separate myself from all the cages that bind me, and the mindset of being caged even after the cages are gone, who would I be? Where would I have the courage to roam, what would become my kingdom, and whose presence would I grace?

I believe that Kalah's life is a metaphor of the transformation Christ longs to bring to you and to me. When we allow Jesus into our lives and accept the forgiveness from sin that he extends to us, the cage door opens wide. But the real transformation comes when we begin to explore this new life. In the process of stepping out, we discover our true selves. We are re-created into the very women God created us to be.

This shedding of cages, this walking out of the bathroom into the wild and wonderful world of God's domain, this discovery of the gift of ourselves is what this book is about. May we as women, as we together move through these pages, come alive to the unique and precious wonder of our lives.

In this process of grasping and living out the identity Christ has created within us, we will discover unique gifts. These gifts are given to us by God, they are knitted within our being. These gifts yearn within us to be brought forth out of darkness into light. They yearn for us to use and express them, even when we are oblivious to their presence within us. As we learn to identify and live from them, our lives will be marked by the kind of energy and freedom and joy I saw in Kalah.

In Romans 8, Paul writes that all of creation is waiting with eager expectation for the sons and daughters of God to be revealed. That is us! The world is waiting with expectation for you and me to be revealed in our full and vibrant glory, using our gifts, creating with passion, healing with love. This too is re-creation.

As Kalah graced my room with her presence and made me long to be more alive, so we, when set free from our cages, awaken in others the longing to be free. In discovering the selves God is calling us to be, we are transformed and brought to life. In being faithful to the claim these gifts place on our lives, we become the hands and feet of Christ. We become agents of transformation. The church of God will be a force to be reckoned with when it becomes a community of women and men exercising and evoking their gifts!

Unfortunately, too many of us go through life unaware of the wild creature within longing for freedom. We are like Kalah in a lidless cage—afraid, unaware, feeling too powerless, weak, or stubborn to leave behind the safety of the boxes which cage us. Our gifts lie latent and unused. Our capacity for joy is bound. While the world hungers on for a taste of true life and freedom, we are in a box hiding in the bathroom.

Why is it so hard to grasp the gifts God has given us and use them to bring beauty to our own lives and the world around us? Why do we as women so easily give up our dreams and callings and refuse to live out the fullness of our potential?

First, self-awareness is a difficult thing to come by. To claim our gifts, we must know who we are, and this takes work. Yet in the struggle to unearth who we are and what we care about, what brings us sadness and what brings us joy, we will discover glimmers of truth about our gifts. The following chapters are designed to facilitate this process. If we seek, we will find.

Second, as women we have historically been cast in the supportive role, particularly in male-female relationships. While this can be a talent in its own right, our history makes us susceptible to overlooking our own gifts, needs, and yearnings in the process of taking care of the people around us.

Likewise, we tend to view the gifts of others as more important and the dreams of others as more possible. Instead of writing that dreamed-about book, going back to school, or taking a class in pottery, we try to satisfy our longings by supporting our husband's career or sending our children to school. After a time, we forget that the longing was ever there. Yet as we begin to speak again of our dreams and visions, as we begin to listen to the message of our lives, clues to our gifts begin to emerge.

There will come a time when you are ready to choose a gift to focus on, roll up your sleeves, and work diligently at using this gift. It is sometimes hard to identify a gift. It can be even harder to use it. We avoid our gifts because recognizing them and using them is work. It takes discipline. And risk. It means giving up the freedom of a thousand different dreams to focus on a few and hone them over time. It means taking ourselves seriously. It means asking others to take ourselves seriously. It means facing the possibility of failure.

If we do nothing but sit in a cage, there is little risk of failure. Yet there is little chance for joy or fulfillment either. Remember the parable of the man who buried the talents given to him for fear he would lose them. If we bury our talents because we are afraid, we will lose the very thing we seek to protect. But if we take the risk of working and developing our gifts, God will be faithful to increase them. And oh, the joy of living out a gift!

Using a gift at times will feel vulnerable and insecure, and the temptation will be to deny the gift to remove the risk. I am reminded of the story of Abraham and Sarah. Sarah was a woman of great character and beauty. She was one of God's greatest blessings to Abraham. Yet how quickly he was ready to betray her in Egypt for the sake of security. Do not underestimate the pull of inertia upon our human spirits.

The remorse that is left after a gift has been betrayed, the sadness of giving away a part of ourselves for the sake of security, is a heavy pain to bear. When we deny our own identities, we will continually be looking outward at other's gifts. We will be threatened by their courage and angered by their success. To disobey the claim gifts make on our life, to settle for some safe middle ground, is to imprison our very souls and destine ourselves to a life of dissatisfaction and envy. But when we experience the true success of simply being and doing that which we were created to be, we will know great peace.

"What is this giftedness written into my being, and how will I use it?" These are the difficult questions, for no one can name your gift for you. People can tell you what they see, and through their eyes you will gain insight. Indeed, part of the importance of a small support group is to have others help you see that which you cannot see.

But ultimately you alone will know when the life you

are living and the things you are investing yourself in have the ring of truth. You must wrestle with your own life, like Jacob wrestled with the angel. When the clarity of truth is upon you, you will know. The voice of God will be all over it. The Holy Spirit will be your guide, and if you wait and search, you will find what God is leading you toward.

Above all, trust in God. Keep your eyes on God, keep your Spirit tuned to God's Spirit, rather than on your own successes or failures. Be obedient to the call God lays on your soul, for God will never ask you to do anything that will weaken or destroy the unique gift God has created in you.

When you are totally at a loss and do not know where even the beginning point is, do not be afraid. The cages of our spirits cannot keep out the healing of God's Spirit. The God who has begun a good work in you will bring it about to completion. With this hope before you, continue the struggle. Do not accept less than this road to freedom and re-creation. For your life is a gift, holy and good in the sight of God.

Blessings, then, as you journey through this book. As you go, I hope you discover the gifts within you, and find the courage to use them with gusto. The world is waiting for the daughters of God to be revealed!

Questions for Reflection

1. What things in life bring you gladness—not mere passing happiness or momentary highs, but a deep-down sense of satisfaction and wholeness? What activities do you love to do? Brainstorm about everything—big and small!

2. What gifts could lay behind your gladness? Look for the themes that run through them. Again, brainstorm. You can sift through and prioritize later.

3. After you've brainstormed, take a break, then come back to your list a day later. What gifts do you see emerging out of the list? Identify one or two specific gifts you can intentionally develop.

4. There are many reasons we deny our gifts. We devalue their worth, we think others can do them better, we don't want to draw attention to ourselves. How do you run from recognizing and exercising your gifts?

5. What are gifts you see in the women in your small group? Write down gifts you have received from each person and share them at the next meeting.

6. Spend time in prayer and meditation this week, asking God to help you live out of your own giftedness. How can you use each gift to bring life, joy, justice, healing to your family, your church, your community?

Suggested Resources

Andrews, William, ed. *Sisters of the Spirit: Three Black Women's Autobiographies of the Nineteenth Century*. Bloomington: Indiana University Press, 1986.

Bozarth, Alla Reneé. *Womanpriest: A Personal Odyssey*. San Diego, Calif.: LuraMedia, 1988.

Leckey, Dolores R. *Women and Creativity*. Mahwah, N.J.: Paulist Press, 1991.

O'Connor, Elizabeth. *The Eighth Day of Creation: Gifts and Creativity*. Waco, Tex.: Word Books, 1971.

Thoele, Sue Patton. *The Woman's Book of Courage*. Berkeley, Calif.: Conari Press, 1991.

2

Women and Christ
Nora O. Lozano-Díaz

Now when Jesus came into the district of Caesarea Philippi, he asked his disciples, "Who do people say that the Son of Man is?" And they said, "Some say John the Baptist, but others Elijah, and still others Jeremiah or one of the prophets." He said to them, "But who do you say that I am?"

Matthew 16:13-15

As a Christian woman, I have struggled often with the question Jesus asked his disciples, "Who do you say that I am?" From a young age, I was taught that Jesus is the Savior of humanity because he died on a cross to bring new life to everybody. In a subtle but strong way, I also was taught that this new life Jesus gives was mainly effective in the spiritual realm of one's existence.

According to this teaching, Jesus was interested in

my spiritual involvement in the church but not in my practical involvement. He did not care if I was hurt every time a man was invited to lead a service and I, as a woman, was overlooked and rejected due to my gender. He did not care about my feelings when, for the same reason, a male pastor denied me the opportunity to run for president of my youth group. These experiences led me to think that Jesus' abounding life would be available to me only in heaven. The church practices were a constant reminder of that.

For a long time I believed all these ideas. But one day a different vision of Jesus and his church was introduced to me. This new vision was full of liberation, compassion, and love! According to it, Jesus did care for my feelings regarding this exclusive society. He was ready to share his abundant life with me, so I, as a woman, could enjoy a more wholistic life here and now. Surprisingly, this Jesus had always been in the Scripture; it was only a matter of discovering him.

According to the Gospels, Jesus was a Jew of the first century. The Jewish society of that time was diverse. In the religious arena, the Jews made room to many different groups such as the priestly establishment, the Pharisees, the Sadducees, the Essenes, and the Qumran branch of the Essene movement. These groups had different political, theological, and cultural views.

In relation to women, the beliefs and practices of these groups were also diverse. Thus it is hard to know the degree of oppression or freedom Jewish women experienced in the first century. However, due to the cultural customs that surrounded the Jewish people, it can be assumed that Jewish women were affected in different degrees, by the patriarchy and sexism of the Greco-Roman world.[1] *Patriarchy* has been defined as a form of community in which the father is the supreme authority in the family. We might say that patriarchy is likewise the form of community in which males are the supreme authority in the town, state, and country. *Sexism* is the doctrine or practice that affirms that one sex is superior to the other one.[2]

The beliefs, practices, and life of Jesus were the inspiration and starting point of another Jewish religious movement. This movement became the foundation of the Christian religion. The biblical scholar Elisabeth Schüssler Fiorenza has done a deep study of the vision, commitment, and praxis of Jesus and his movement. She has concluded that two notions were basic in the Jesus movement—the concept of God and the vision of the kingdom *(basileia).*[3]

In the Jesus movement, God was seen in a different way than the exclusivistic traditional one.

> The Jesus movement articulates a quite different understanding of God because it had experienced in the praxis of Jesus a God who called not Israel's righteous and pious but its religiously deficient and its social underdogs. In the ministry of Jesus God is experienced as all-inclusive love, letting the sun shine and the rain fall equally on the righteous and on sinners (Matt. 5:45). This God is a God of graciousness and goodness who accepts everyone and brings about justice and well-being for everybody without exception. The creator God accepts all members of Israel, and especially the impoverished, the crippled, the outcast, the sinners and prostitutes, as long as they are prepared to engage in the perspective and power of the *basileia.*[4]

In Jesus' teachings the kingdom of God, the *basileia,* was seen as a tension between present and future. He proclaimed that the present coming of the kingdom was an opportunity to become whole in this current life. Every time Jesus shared his beliefs, healed someone, cast out a demon, challenged the unjust social structures of his time, or invited the uninvited, the *basileia* of God was experienced on earth. The *basileia* vision of Jesus meant an opportunity for the unclean, the crippled, the sinners, and the socially marginalized to become whole persons.[5]

> The *basileia* vision of Jesus makes people whole, healthy, cleansed, and strong. It restores people's humanity and life. The salvation of the *basileia* is not confined to the soul but spells wholeness for the total person in her/his social relations.[6]

Jesus experienced an all-inclusive, loving God who created everybody as equals and who is full of goodness and graciousness. Jesus understood the vision of the kingdom of God as a realm where everybody has an opportunity to become whole and to experience a better existence. This perception of God and the kingdom led him to create an inclusive movement in which everybody was invited, welcomed, and accepted under the same terms, spiritually as well as practically. This includes children, women and men, and people of diverse races as well as of different social/economic conditions. This inclusive Jesus movement has been called by Fiorenza "the discipleship of equals." And Fiorenza has regarded the women in this movement as "women's powerful heritage."[7]

The first time I read about this inclusive movement,

I wondered, but where are the women of this movement? Since I was little I was taught many stories about the men around Jesus, but I hardly remember hearing any stories about the women around Jesus.

It is true that there are more stories in the Bible about the men around Jesus. But it is also true that the stories about the women around Jesus have been overlooked throughout history. As women, we need to recover them![8] These stories are our powerful heritage, because they show us how Jesus had a special interest in women. He included them in his ministry, not only as members but also as leaders. He gave them more complete lives physically, emotionally, and spiritually. But these stories are also our powerful heritage because they tell us about strong women who demanded healing for themselves or their family members; about faithful women disciples who accompanied Jesus throughout his whole ministry; about wise and spiritual women who discussed the issues of the kingdom with Jesus; about committed women who were called to share and preach the good news of the kingdom of God; and about brave women who followed Jesus in the most crucial times of his life. The following stories are an example of this powerful heritage:

Jesus and the woman sick of a chronic hemorrhage

The woman in Mark 5:25-34 had been suffering from bleeding for twelve years. She had spent all her money trying to get better. But nothing had cured her. Furthermore, her suffering was even worse because this sickness automatically marked her as unclean and set her

apart from "regular" people. According to Leviticus
15:19, any person who touched a woman with such sickness would also be unclean. For this reason, it was impossible for the woman to approach Jesus in a public
way.

So in silence she drew near to Jesus and tried to
touch at least his garment. Jesus recognized that power
had left him. When he asked the crowd what had happened, he learned that a bleeding woman had touched
him. Instead of getting angry at her for making him unclean, Jesus talked to the woman and healed her completely. Furthermore, Jesus praised her for her faith and
finally dismissed her in peace.

In this story, Jesus showed much concern and compassion for the unclean woman, and the woman showed
much courage in approaching Jesus. That day the *basileia* of God, the wholeness of Jesus, became present and
changed forever the life of this woman.

Jesus and Martha and Mary

In John 11:5-27 and Luke 10:38-42, we see that Jesus
loved Martha and Mary. These passages show the deep
relationship that existed between Jesus and these two
women. Jesus did not have only a relationship with them,
he had a friendship with them. He spent time visiting
with them, talking about different topics, and without a
doubt discussing spiritual matters. In John 11:20-27,
Martha and Jesus had a deep spiritual conversation in
which Jesus disclosed to her that he was the resurrection
and the life. In response to Jesus' words, Martha articu-
lated a christological confession that became fundamen-
tal in the Gospel of John, "Yes, Lord, I believe that you

are the Messiah, the Son of God, the one coming into the world."

This confession is the same one Peter made in Matthew 16:13-20. The confessions of Martha and Peter were revealed to them by the gracious God of Jesus, who draws no distinction between men and women and who calls both to an equal ministry.

Jesus and the discipleship of women

Luke 8:1-3 mentions that while Jesus was traveling around the different cities and villages, proclaiming and bringing the good news of the kingdom of God, the twelve disciples and many women were with him. Among these women were Joanna, the wife of Herod's steward Chuza, Susanna, and Mary, called Magdalene. These women were faithful followers of Jesus. Their commitment to Jesus and his movement was so great that they decided to stay with Jesus during the time of his crucifixion, burial, and resurrection. These faithful and courageous women stayed by him even through his darkest hour (Matt. 27:45-61, Mark 15:33-47, Luke 23:26-56, John 19:23-29). Furthermore, the discipleship of women seems to have been so strong and solid that after Jesus' resurrection, the women were privileged to see him first and to receive the commandment to go as witness of the resurrection (Matt. 28:1-10, Mark 16:1-10, and John 20:11-18). Given the respect, dignity, love, and wholeness women received from Jesus, it does not come as a surprise that they decided to follow Jesus during all his ministry, even to the point of risking their own physical well-being.

These stories, and many others in the Gospels, are

our powerful heritage because they challenge us to be strong, persistent, wise, brave, spiritual, faithful, and committed, just as our foremothers. They invite us to ask the gracious God of Jesus for complete healing for our lives. They call us to experience a life of wholeness, here and now.

This new vision of Jesus and the women around him has become a source of security and strength in my life. Security because now I know that even though the Christian church has been permeated with patriarchal and sexist influences, the original church that Jesus envisioned was against these influences. The Jesus movement intended to be an equal place for *all* of the children of God. The present church should strive to be such an equal place too. This new vision is also a source of strength because it empowers me to continue the journey toward the wholeness, the *basileia,* that Jesus designed for me as a woman.

When Jesus touched the lives of the women in the Gospels, he called them to a new beginning, to a new life of wholeness. In the same way, Jesus is calling us today to a new and better life.

The decision is ours. May the gracious God of Jesus grant us the courage to decide to choose freedom, face challenges, and begin to make life-changing actions. Amen!

Questions for Reflection

1. What stories did you hear about Jesus when you were growing up? What is the picture of Jesus that emerges from these stories?

2. Does a different vision of Jesus emerge for you

from this chapter? If so, what are the characteristics of this new vision?

3. The women around Jesus were portrayed as strong, wise, spiritual, committed, and brave. Is this women's image new for you? Does it present you with any challenges?

4. These women had to make crucial decisions to become whole. What decisions do you need to make to start or to continue your journey toward wholeness?

5. Give thanks for the stage in which you are right now as a woman. Celebrate being on your way to becoming more complete.

Suggested Resources

Fiorenza, Elisabeth Schüssler. *In Memory of Her.* New York: The Crossroad Publishing Company, 1985.

Mac Haffie, Barbara J. *Her Story.* Philadelphia: Fortress Press, 1986.

Moltmann-Wendel, Elisabeth. *The Women Around Jesus.* New York: the Crossroad Publishing Company, 1990.

Wahlbert, Rachel Conrad. *Jesus and the Freed Woman.* New York: Paulist Press, 1978.

3

Women and the Image of God

Nora O. Lozano-Díaz

> . . . as I explained before, the woman does not possess the image of God in herself, but only when taken together with the male who is her head, so the whole substance is one image. . . . But as far as the man is concerned, he is by himself alone the image of God. . . .
>
> *Augustine*

*I*n *Theology from the Womb of Asia*, C. S. Song reflects on the creation story and invites us to see the word *image* not as a noun but as a verb. If we see image as action, Song continues, we will see that God imagined us out of God's own self. Moreover, God envisioned *all the created things* in relation to God's own self.[1]

Unfortunately, as human beings, we have reversed the process and have imagined God according to our own image. Our limited vision has forced us to see God through our values—those characteristics and elements most important to us. Through history, this process of imagining God according to the values of a certain group or society has been common. In a matriarchal society, God has been a woman; in a patriarchal group, God has been a man; in a black population, God has been black; and in a Hispanic country, God has spoken Spanish.

But at this point it is pertinent to ask who determines the values of a group. Usually the values are formed by those who are in power, according to their own image and perception of the world. During biblical times Jewish culture was patriarchal and men were in power. Therefore the deity was pictured mainly as a man and in masculine roles, such as father, lord, king, son, warrior.

Something similar has happened in today's world, since Christianity has been transmitted through patriarchal societies in which the Western perception of the world has been dominant. The official image of God has been as a white male.

For humankind, the concept of God has shaped a vast part of our reality and the way that we relate as persons of different gender and race. Consequently, picturing God according to one specific image conveys a series of issues worth examining.

The first problem resides in the fact that one specific image of God seems to allow God to become private property, which embodies power. This works in the following way: if God reflects exclusively the characteristics

of a certain group, leaving out the rest of the world population, then God seems to be like the members of that
elite group and to think like them.

This perception gives people room to say, "If God is
like me, then I know God perfectly, and I can interpret
God's will for the rest of the people that are different than
God and me." If, for instance, God is a white male, wom-
en and ethnic groups are inferior. They are not like God.
They do not reflect God's image. In consequence, white
men, as God's representatives on earth, have to tell them
how to manage their lives.

A second problem of picturing God according to
one specific image is that whoever does this commits
idolatry. Idolatry is the worship of idols. Am I worshiping
myself when I picture God exactly like me? Am I trying to
be like God to have power and control over others? Is patriarchy fostering idolatry by making an idol of all men,
and allowing only one masculine image of God?

Rosemary Radford Ruether says,

> Patriarchy itself must fall under the biblical denunciations
> of idolatry and blasphemy, the idolizing of the male as
> representative of divinity. It is idolatrous to make males
> more "like God" than females. It is blasphemous to use
> the image and name of the Holy to justify patriarchal
> domination and law.[2]

A third and final problem of envisioning God according to one particular image is that this limits the freedom of God. God as God cannot be totally measured or
controlled by any image or perception, because God in
God's mystery transcends all of them.[3]

The use of any sole image of God will limit the free

nature of the divine. This is the case when only masculine imagery is used to picture God. Traditionally, God
has been depicted with conventional male characteristics
and attributes, such as power, strength, rationality, order,
novelty, transformation, dominion, and control. Recently
some conventional female characteristics—such as care,
compassion, nurture, preservation, empathy, receptivity,
and suffering—have been attributed to God. Yet the traditional vision of a masculine God has obscured the nature of the divine one who created male and female in
God's own image and as equal partners.

If we truly believe that God created male and female
in God's own image, then we cannot support an exclusive and limited vision of God. Moreover, we cannot accept a male image of God that has received characteristics and attributes the patriarchal system conceived in its
mind. Who has determined that men are to be rational,
powerful, or in control—and that women are to be recep-
tive, caring, and compassionate?[4]

If these roles have just been a maneuver of fallen
societal systems, then we must challenge them. And if
these roles have been assigned to a male God to prove
the superiority of men and the inferiority of women, then
we must reject them.

Since the traditional image of God has been primarily male, we need to look for more inclusive images of
God. These images should present a God that is male
and female, powerful and compassionate, caring and rational, passive and active, a God who affirms and reflects
not just one segment of the population but all of God's
creation.

Fortunately, the Bible gives room to see God in different ways and with diverse characteristics and attributes. God was seen by David as king and warrior, by Isaiah as peace, by Solomon as wisdom, by Moses as mother, and by the psalmist as rock and fortress. Due to our patriarchal world, some of the images of God that have been neglected the most are female ones. As women, it can be very healing to explore these female images of God.

The strongest female image of God in the Bible is as mother. In Numbers 11:12, Moses and God had a conversation in which Moses pictured God as Israel's mother and wet nurse. It is interesting to connect this verse with the words in Deuteronomy 34:10. There Moses appears as the prophet God knew face to face. If indeed God and Moses were involved in this close relationship, Moses' picture of God as mother helps disclose the womanhood of God. Other references to God as mother are found in the writings of the prophet Isaiah, who depicts God as a woman in labor (42:14) and as the one who carried Israel from the womb (46:3-4).

In the book of Proverbs, Wisdom is referred to as a female character which is a part of God. Although Wisdom may be seen as an attribute of God, Wisdom is also found as co-creator with God (8:22-31) and as a female figure who has her own personality, voice, and actions (1:20-33 and 8:1-21). By no means am I saying that Wisdom is another God, but that Wisdom is the female dimension of God.

Finally, in the New Testament Jesus pictured God as the woman who rejoices when she finds her lost coin (Luke 15:8-10). It is important to note that, in spite of the patriarchal system, this Jesus (who was so close to God) used a feminine image for God.

The point in recovering the female image of God is not to prove that God is a woman—and so reverse patriarchal oppression—but to affirm that God is male and female yet also neither. Through a vision of a more wholistic God, we will recover some of the characteristics lost when God was declared a white male with masculine roles and activities.

To reject the divided image of God will mean freedom from many of the stereotypes women and men have had to bear during their lives. For instance, God is a God who makes decisions and answers "Yes," "Wait," or "No." Men as images of this male God have been taught to be in control of themselves and make their own decisions by likewise saying "Yes," "Wait," or "No." In contrast, women are often taught to say "Yes" but have a hard time making decisions or saying "Wait" or "No."

Another dimension we need to recover as women is the right to be active subjects in and not passive objects of history. Again, men as the image of the male God who is creator of history, have been raised to be subjects of history. But women, as beings far from portraying the image of God, have been taught to be objects.

Freeing the image of God from all its many distortions can change human attitudes and actions. This transformation will bring respect and equality among all human beings—regardless of gender, race, color, or language.

Finally, the use of varied images of God will help remind us that God cares not only for us but for all the creation because it was made by God's hands and in God's own image.

Questions for Reflection

1. Try to pray or talk to God imagining God in a different way from the one you were taught. Maybe you can use a female image of God.

2. Write your reactions, thoughts, or feelings regarding imagining God in a different way from the one you were taught.

3. Which other images of God can you use?

4. Write some other attributes or characteristics of God that women have lost due to the use of a male image of God. Think of attributes or characteristics that you have not embraced as consequence of the division of sex roles.

5. After identifying the traits mentioned in the previous question, think of ways to apply these characteristics in your daily life.

Suggested Resources

Christ, Carol and Plaskow, Judith. *Weaving the Visions: New Patterns in Feminist Spirituality.* New York: Harper & Row, Publishers, 1989.

Clanton, Jann Aldredge. *In Whose Image?* New York: The Crossroad Publishing Company, 1990.

Johnson, Elizabeth A. "The Incomprehensibility of God and the Image of God Male and Female." *Theological Studies* 45 (September 1984): 441-465

Radford Ruether, Rosemary. *Sexism and God Talk.* Boston: Beacon Press, 1983.

Schneiders, Sandra M. *Women and the Word.* Mahwah: N.J.: Paulist Press, 1986.

4

Women and Spirituality
Anne Baxter

> *H*one and spread your spirit, till you yourself are a sail, whetted, translucent, broadside to the merest puff.
>
> *Annie Dillard*

*W*hen I was a junior at my evangelical Christian liberal arts college, my friends and I discovered a certain breed of men—the "spiritual giants." Nice looking in a predictable way, clean-cut, well-spoken, morally upright, disciplined, with a heart for God and a desire to spread the gospel of Christ, they floated to the top of the student body and lay over us like a thick layer of cream.

The spiritual giants volunteered for student mission projects and were asked to be leaders the following year. They were asked to pray in chapel and lead student worship. They were interested in overseas missions and

planned on going to seminary. They prayed together reg-
ularly. They were the leaders of tomorrow, the future of
the evangelical tradition. Few of them dated, for women
were a distraction which would prevent them from fully
carrying out the call to greatness which God had stamped
on their lives.

My friends and I also cared about God and living the
gospel. We too were involved in internships and mission
projects. But no one asked us to lead a chapel. No one
hailed us as the future of the evangelical tradition. We
never talked about the discrepancy. It was a given. We
were women.

Yet the situation rankled somewhere within, for we
mocked the shiny surface of these upstanding giants.
And underneath our sarcasm lay an almost undetectable
shame, undetectable because it was so much a part of
our identity as women that we were barely aware it existed. It was a shame that maybe they were right. That maybe they were the giants of the spirit and we were the
grasshoppers, stretching only to their knee-caps at our
highest jump. That maybe they would forever be the men
after God's heart, while we remained destined help-
mates of their vision.

For so long men like this have stood as the ideal expression of Christian spirituality. Spiritual excellence required being morally upright and disciplined, untainted
by the blood and guts of daily life and unconcerned with
its more trivial details. It meant leaving behind worldly
pursuits to boldly and courageously carry out the mission
of God. It required being a soldier of the cross, forging
pathways through legions of evil with the two-edged
sword, so women and children could pass safely through.

It meant being a leader—brave, strong, single-mindedly pursuing what is just and right.

For better or for worse, these qualities have been assigned to our greatest heroes of the Christian faith. They have become the legacy of what it means in popular Christendom to excel spiritually.

For the most part, men have been responsible for interpreting the lives of our heroes and shaping the definitions of our faith. Ironically, women have been discouraged from expressing the very qualities that men traditionally lift up as heroic and spiritual. Women are not to be leaders, but followers. Women are not bravely to adhere to an inner conviction of what is right, but to submit to moral decisions handed down by external authorities.

The value of a woman lies not in her ability to single-mindedly carry out the mission of God, but in her capacity to think and dress and act and feel in ways acceptable and enjoyable to the rest of society—especially men. Usually she achieves this by submerging her identity, needs, and interests to support, encourage, or take on someone else's identity, needs, and interests.

We who are women find ourselves in a no-win situation. We are continually exposed to and measure ourselves by a male-formed ideal of spirituality. Yet we are told that we as women either cannot or should not live up to that ideal.

What spiritual ideal has the church left to us as women? If we as women are subtly and not-so-subtly discouraged from the realm of bold leading and proactive partnership in the work of God, what ideal *are* we to aspire toward? We have been handed a spirituality defined not by leadership but by submission.

While material on spirituality has been written through the ages that is both profoundly challenging and insistently balanced, such views have not often been reflected in the more popular expressions of Christianity. In expressions of Christianity that have been heavily wed to societal norms, the church has upheld a neat double-standard in the area of spirituality.

The ideal expression of the Christian life for a man is to be an active defender of and partner in the very mission of God. "Follow me, and I will make you fishers of men." "Proclaim the good news. Cure the sick, raise the dead, cleanse the lepers, cast out demons." "Make disciples of all nations." "All authority on heaven and earth has been given to you." "We are ambassadors for Christ." "Let your light shine before others." "Keep alert, stand firm in your faith, be courageous, be strong." "Convince, rebuke, and encourage." "Do not fear those who can kill the body." "Beware of the dogs, beware of the evil workers, beware of those who mutilate the flesh!" "See to it that no one takes you captive through philosophy and empty deceit." "Fight the good fight of faith." "Hold fast to what we have attained."

These activities, when exalted and lived out without a spirit of love, obedience, compassion, and humility, too easily become demonic. They become expressions of an oppressive and victimizing desire for power and control. It is not the mission of God that is furthered, but the mission of men.

For a woman, the ideal expression of the Christian faith, shaped by a patriarchal definition of the female role and legitimated by the church, is submitting to external demands, serving those around her, and protecting the peace of the community. "Wives, be subject to your husbands." "Clothe yourself with compassion, kindness, humility, meekness, and patience." "Never avenge yourself." "Do not judge." "Live peaceably with all." "Love your enemy." "If you are angry, you will be liable for judgment." "Forgive, and you will be forgiven." "Bear with one another in love, making every effort to maintain the unity of the Spirit." "Turn your other cheek." "Be perfect."

Such words, when removed from the context of self-defined, integrated personhood, become crippling half-truths which pour condemnation on women. Binding our tongues and imprisoning our souls, they too become expressions of the demonic. Women end up submitting not to the ways of God but to the ways of men.

I believe we have yet to understand fully the overwhelming and pervasive cost to both men and women of such a dichotomy. Over and over we find women in the church who have been taught that selfless love is virtuous, that sacrificing one's own well-being to satisfy another is the call of Christ. The result is women in great pain; women plagued by perfectionism, fear, depression, guilt, addictive relationships; women unable fully to love themselves or others.

Anne Wilson Schafe, in *Co-Dependence: Misunderstood—Mistreated*, writes about the connection between the pervasive "disease" of co-dependency and the woman still defined by the roles laid upon her by society.

> She gets her identity completely from outside herself; she has no self-esteem or self-worth; she is isolated from her feelings; and she spends much of her time trying to figure

out what others want so she can give it to them. She is
lonely because she is estranged from herself. She is con-
trolling because she has no self and is so dependent upon
others. . . . The non-liberated woman and the co-
dependent person is the same person.[1]

Schafe sees sexism and co-dependency as expressions of
a disease she calls the addictive process, which is inherent in our societal system.

Christian spirituality as traditionally modeled in the
church is both an expression of and an upholder of the
addictive process. When we let this system define the
way we live, we become walking shells, not fully human,
not fully alive. We become stunted not only in our relationship to the self and others but in our relationship
with God.

We don't know how to be honest with God, for we
don't know how to be honest with ourselves. We don't
trust our own unique way of encountering God which is
so vital for our spiritual health. So we let forces outside us
define our expression of faith. We don't know the joy of
being fully accepted by God because we hide our brokenness to fulfill, with a false flourish of perfection, the
role society assigns us.

Jesus said, "I have come that you might have life,
and have it more abundantly." If what we have been per-
ceiving as the call of Christ to women brings death to our
selves, death to our relationships, death to our family and
society, and death to our relationship with God, then I
am convinced we are not experiencing the call of Christ.
We are experiencing the imprisonment of the demonic.

Women must begin to discover within the biblical
text a meaning of spirituality which brings us healing.

Only after facing up to our own pain and imprisonment can we be agents of change in the world around us. This is, I believe, a matter of life and death, not only for us, but for our families, our society, and our world.

One point of departure for this new understanding of spirituality lies in the word *wholeness*. Christian spirituality embraces the whole of life—how we relate to our bodies, our families, our society, our earth; what authorities we choose to submit to and why; when we fulfill the desires of others and when we fulfill our own; whose definition of God, womanhood, and spirituality we live by. It is as we struggle with life in all its complexity that we encounter the wholeness, beauty, truth, and wisdom of Christ.

Renewed through the encounter, empowered by the Spirit, we ourselves are ushered into wholeness of the divine. Each of our journeys will be different as we seek to discover the woman God created us to be. But each of us must face the insecurity of her chosen road. And each of us must overcome the temptation to settle for that which is safe, comfortable, and ultimately far, far less.

My journey has included overcoming unhealthy patterns of relating; learning to trust my inner voice and speak it with integrity; embracing my sexuality as a precious gift and protecting it from exploitation; and taking responsibility for my emotional, physical, and spiritual health. But perhaps more than anything else, I am learning to be honest with God. "God, this is who I am. This is what I've done, and this is what I ought to have done. This is what you are, though, and thank heavens for that."

I stand up to God and therefore to the world and say

"I AM. . . . THIS IS WHO I AM." When the dust settles, God hasn't gone anywhere nor has the world. And who I am is okay. Ultimately, it is not I who heal myself. Though I don't like to admit it, for I work hard for wholeness, I am powerless to heal the brokenness that plagues me. The new life I sense stirring within me—which ultimately *is* me—is a gift of grace, formed out of the very chaos of my life. In my shouts of honesty I receive the gift of self. Such grace is a mystery to me.

When Jesus came, he offered his people freedom and liberation from an exclusive and legalistic spirituality. They found his liberation oppressive, for it called them to let go of all they had identified as worthy and upright and good. Unable to stand the discomfort of the mystery, they killed him.

Let it be known: each day Christ comes to us and extends the same mystery. It is never too late to receive it. Each day is a new beginning if we so choose. Each day we must choose the beginning anew. Choose wisely. The matter, I believe, is one of life and death.

Questions for Reflection

1. Reflecting on your life, seek to identify the qualities of "spiritual excellence" you were taught to emulate. What have been the positive and negative effects of this system?

2. Part of the healing of our concepts of spirituality comes as we choose for ourselves new role models for a life of faith. Who can be a role model for you in your spiritual journey? What qualities attract you to this person's life?

3. One day my mother shared with me an experi-

ence she had of God. She was washing cranberries in the kitchen sink. The berries—firm, buoyant, shiny—were tightly packed across the clear, cold surface of the water. Light reflected off their hard skins. Each had its own unique combination of reds. Some were deep like burgundy wine, others light like cherry punch. Their bright, buoyancy filled my mother with a sense of gratitude so pungent it almost made her cry. My mother kept this experience quiet for years. She felt ashamed by her reaction to beauty and somehow inadequate for not seeing God in the "usual" way.

Part of reclaiming our own spirituality as women is to discover and celebrate our own unique ways of meeting God. In what ways does God encounter you most potently? How does God come to you in the ordinary moments of your day?

4. Identify the broken points in your life in need of healing. What are the areas that trip you up over and over? Where do you feel the most vulnerable, the most afraid? Meditate on the love of God embracing, forgiving, and accepting you as you are.

5. While God loves us as we are, God also gives us the gift of new beginnings. What beginnings do you feel God calling you to take? How is this broader understanding of spirituality calling you out of hiding?

6. How can the support group help you in these new beginnings?

Suggested Resources

Bakson, Marjory Zoet. *Braided Streams: Esther and a Woman's Way of Growing.* San Diego: Luria Media, 1985.

Bozarth, All Renee. *Love's Prism: Reflections from the Heart of a*

Woman. Kansas City: Sheed and Ward, 1987.

Chervin, Ronda and Neill, Mary. *The Woman's Tale: A Journal of Inner Exploration*. New York: The Seabury Press, 1980.

Conn, Joann Wolski, ed. *Women's Spirituality: Resources for Christian Development*. New York: Paulist Press, 1988.

Each Day a New Beginning: Daily Meditations for Women. Hazeldon Meditation Series, San Francisco: Harper & Row, 1982.

Fischer, Kathleen. *Women at the Well: Feminist Perspectives on Spiritual Direction*. New York: Paulist Press, 1988.

Gilligan, Carol. *In a Different Voice*. Cambridge: Harvard University Press, 1982.

Schaef, Anne Wilson. *Co-Dependence: Misunderstood—Mistreated*. San Francisco: Harper & Row, 1986.

Valentine, Mary Hester. *Saints for Contemporary Women*. Chicago: Thomas More Press, 1987.

5

Women and Their Learning Styles
Helen Havlik

*I*n describing their lives, women commonly [talk] about voice and silence: "speaking up," "speaking out," "being silenced," "not being heard," "really listening," "really talking," "words as weapons," "feeling deaf and dumb," "having no words," "saying what you mean," "listening to be heard," and so on in an endless variety of connotations all having to do with sense of mind, self-worth, and feelings of isolation from or connection to others . . . women repeatedly [use] the metaphor of voice to depict their intellectual and ethical development; and that the development of a sense of voice, mind, and self [are] intricately intertwined.

Women's Ways of Knowing

I clearly remember my first flash of personal inspiration at age thirteen. I was on a camping trip with my Girl Scout troop. It was a rainy, miserable day. Everyone else was doing crafts. Not that I didn't like crafts, but I wasn't interested that day, so I was aimlessly wandering around the troop house, alternately looking at the other girls' projects and staring out the window.

Then, for the first time in my life, a poem came into my mind. Not one I had read before, but my *own* poem. One *I* was making out of my own mind, my own experience. I found a piece of paper and began writing,

> The rain came down in sheets of shimmer
> and even the moon had lost its glimmer.
> The mosses on the wet black ground
> took shape and color, all around. . . .

There's more, but the point is not what came out. The point is that the words were *mine*, my own words in my own voice.

Later, as a fifteen-year-old, I had my first experience of challenging authority. This was not easy for a girl brought up to be obedient (though I had my stubborn streak) and afraid of transgressing the rules.

I awoke in the middle of a Friday night with an excruciating pain in my abdomen. I couldn't get up to get my parents, so I moaned until my sister woke up and went downstairs to them. They called the doctor (a higher authority than they). He said something like, "It's nothing—give her a hot water bottle and it will go away." Following his advice, they handed me a hot water bottle and told me to go back to sleep.

Now in my family, there is an often-repeated story of

how my grandfather's twin brother died at age nine because his parents unknowingly put a hot water bottle on his painful abdomen and his appendix ruptured, sending toxins throughout his body. I lay there in the dark, knowing that story, knowing I was supposed to obey authority figures, and knowing I had appendicitis.

How I knew I had appendicitis, I can't say. Maybe I had heard the symptoms on TV or someone I knew had been through it. But somehow I mustered the courage to follow my intuition and not use the water bottle. It was a long night.

The next day, still in pain, I was taken to the doctor (who was surprised I really was in pain), then the hospital. There the surgeon said it probably was just a ruptured ovary. In the operating room they discovered an appendix so swollen it would have ruptured in another half hour.

It has been assumed for the last century or so that women learn to think (if at all) as men do. Several important studies about "human" development have drawn important conclusions about the way "people" grow intellectually, morally and psychologically. These studies have influenced everything from the way classrooms are run, to popular culture and women's "natural" roles.

The trouble with such studies is that

> until recently women have played only a minor role as theorists in the social sciences. The authors of the major theories of human development have been men . . . women have been missing even as research subjects. . . .[1]

Society has assumed—and women have internalized—the notion that the male way is the norm.

In 1982, however, Carol Gilligan challenged the status quo. She had the audacity to use women and girls as
research subjects. She found that the major studies of
Piaget (1965) and Kohlberg (1981, 1984) in the area of
moral development contrasted sharply with her findings
with women. This research set the stage for major
changes in how social scientists see women and men. It
opened the door for women to "speak up," to be heard
in ways we never dreamed possible.[2]

In 1986, Mary Field Belenky, Blythe McVicker Clin-
chy, Nancy Rule Goldberger, and Jill Mattuck Tarule published *Women's Ways of Knowing: The Development of
Self, Voice and Mind.* Inspired by Gilligan's research,
these women, all involved in some way with education,
created a research project to see if women develop intellectually the same way men do. They identified seven
"ways of knowing" that seemed common to the women
they interviewed. They concluded that women do seem
to develop differently than men. They noted that some
women, depending on circumstances, never reach their
potential in terms of self, voice, and intellect, apparently
because our systems of education are male-biased and
the socialization of girls tends to silence them.

Here is a summary of the seven stages of knowing
identified in *Women's Ways of Knowing. Silence* is the
first way of knowing. It is that place where women have
been traditionally through history. "Shut up!" "You're
just a woman, you don't know what you're talking
about." "We don't publish books by women." These are
ways we have been enjoined to keep silent. The destruc-
tion of human potential and souls has been enormous
because of this conspiracy of silence. It allows for wife

abuse, child abuse, and child sexual abuse. This is because "He really means well. After all, he's the man and he knows best. If I keep my mouth shut, he won't leave me—it's worth a few bruises to have a man around."

At some point, women begin to *listen* to the voices of others, which is a second way of knowing one step beyond mere silence. My first poem, so reminiscent of Stevenson's work, was a response to his voice, an echoing in my own mind of what poetry should be. We learn to know that our teachers, our parents, our doctors—any authority figure, in fact (the so-called "experts")—have the answers. If we pay attention to them everything will be all right. Many women never move beyond this stage of development.

The third and fourth ways of knowing are called *subjective knowledge*. They take a woman into herself for wisdom and guidance. Many women come to such knowledge in college or post-college years, when they begin to know that they do have personal insight and intuition. Their inner voices begin to demand attention and get it. This is the beginning of challenging authority as the final expert. Women become their own best experts and trust themselves even when they seem to be outside the mainstream of thought. Often this stage becomes extreme, to the point where outside information is a threat. Subjective knowledge tends to be based on feelings and intuitions. Many women stay in this stage of development for most of their lives.

Because of our educational system, women come into contact with *procedural knowledge* at some point. This is the "voice of reason," which often becomes overdeveloped in women trying to fit into a patriarchal system. But it is a necessary part of development, balancing the pure subjectivity of inner voices. The voice of reason comes from the outside to say "Get the facts, ma'am." We hear this voice demanding an outline for that research paper, rather than letting the words come as they will.

A difference in female development comes at stage six, which is labeled *separate and connected knowing*. This is the time of a women's life when she begins questioning everything and takes nothing for granted. Thinking becomes systematic and women (especially in higher education) learn to play the game according to the male rules. Connected knowing, on the other hand, has to do with empathy—the ability to connect with people emotionally and not just intellectually.

The challenge for women is to take the separate and connected ways of knowing that most of us have come to, and integrate them. It is not enough to base everything on other people's opinions—we must have our own. It is not enough for us to be strictly objective, denying our emotional, intuitive sides for the sake of impartiality and conventionality. It is not enough just to empathize without some critical thinking going on as well.

The integration of the voices becomes what these authors call *constructivist thinking*—the seventh stage of development. This is

> a refreshing mixture of idealism and realism. . . . Constructivist women aspire to work that contributes to the empowerment and improvement in the quality of the life of others. . . . Their desire [is] to have "a room of their own," as Virginia Woolf calls it, in a family and community and world that they helped make livable.[3]

The challenge for us is to see the facts of our own development clearly and to help other women in their own quest for self-actualization. A voice is a precious thing to waste.

Questions for Reflection

1. Think back on your life. Try to identify experiences in which you were aware of using your own voice. Did you make a stand for yourself? Did you question the status quo?

2. When have you been silenced? As a child, how free were you to voice your ideas, opinions, and feelings in your family? When were you most silent?

3. In which situations, and around what kind of people, is it hard for you speak?

4. Has your experience of intellectual development been similar or different from the way Belenky, et al., describe it?

5. In what settings has learning been most exciting and productive for you?

Suggested Resources

Belenky, Mary Field, et al. *Women's Ways of Knowing: The Development of Self, Voice and Mind*. New York: Basic Books, Inc., 1986. (This book contains an extended bibliography, so anyone interested in further reading can use that as a guideline.)

Gilligan, Carol. *In a Different Voice: Psychological Theory and Women's Development*. Cambridge: Harvard University Press, 1982.

Harris, Maria. *Women and Teaching*. Mahwah, N.J.: Paulist Press, 1988.

6

Women and Their Families
Carol M. Schreck

A Parable

Once upon a time a baby girl was born. Her name was Elizabeth. Elizabeth was unlike anyone who had lived before or would live again. She was priceless, incomparable, a trillion-dollar diamond in the rough.

For the first two years of life, Elizabeth only knew herself from the reflections she saw in the eyes of her caretakers. Unfortunately, Elizabeth's caretakers, although not blind, had glasses over their eyes. Each set of glasses had an image on the lens. Consequently each caretaker saw Elizabeth according to the image on the glasses through which she or he looked at her.

Thus, even though her caretakers were physically present, not one of them ever actually saw *her*. By the time Elizabeth was an adult, she had become a mosaic of other people's images of her, none of which reflected who she truly was.

Sometimes at night, when she was all alone, Elizabeth sensed that something crucial was missing. She experienced this as a gnawing emptiness—a deep void. Elizabeth tried to fill the emptiness and void with possessions, exercise, food, money, prestige, chemicals, sex, children, relationships, productivity, religious experience, caregiving, fantasies, success, and endless efforts to be a very good, kind person.

But no matter what she did, the gnawing emptiness remained. On one occasion in the quiet of the night, when all the distractions ceased and Elizabeth had fallen into a deep sleep, she had a dream.

In a distant room was a pale, fragile child huddled on a small, worn cot in the dark. Elizabeth tried to ignore her by bolting the door and busying herself with husband, children, and the unending list of commitments that accompanied each new day. Occasionally, however, when a lull quieted the incessant clamor of the urgent, Elizabeth heard the barely audible call of the small child locked away.

The dream shifted and Elizabeth found herself standing at the graveside of that little girl. Waves of sadness swept over her as she read her own name on the tombstone.

Elizabeth
Age Eight
Death Due to Neglect and
Failure to Thrive

Grief-stricken and startled, Elizabeth fled to the distant room. She unbolted and threw open the door. Rushing to the cot, she carefully lifted the frail child. Her eyes frantically searched for some sign of life in the small, limp body. Enfolding the child in her arms, Elizabeth sobbed with remorse, fearful that she had come too late and that her child had died. Elizabeth felt certain that the gnawing emptiness would totally engulf her. A feeble stirring of the child snatched Elizabeth back from the edge of the dark abyss. Ever so faintly, the child whispered, "I thought you'd never come."[1]

A child knows herself during the early developmental years only through the reflections she observes in the eyes of her caretakers. These caretakers are parents and relatives who often view their child through "glasses" clouded by the images of their own unfulfilled expectations and needs.

Even the initial task of naming a daughter may communicate certain hopes and dreams of her mother or father. Perhaps her parents desire that she embody the virtues of Great Aunt Katherine, or the artistic talent of Grandmother Abigail. Sometimes a guilt-ridden parent, attempting to rework unfinished business with her or his deceased mother, will name a daughter after that parent.

Most women have never taken the time to research the history of their given names. Such information can shed light on the unspoken expectations that parents carried for her and which they attempted to cultivate as part of the mosaic of her person.

Coming to know and understand one's parents, grandparents, and other relatives from an adult perspective helps to sharpen a woman's understanding of her self. Certain rules are transmitted by the family through the generations. Often family members give blind obedience to such rules, never questioning their purpose and value.

For example, affixed to every pair of Sutherland-family glasses is the rule that "Sutherland women are self-sacrificing, submissive helpers whose identity is defined by their relationships to husbands and children." Therefore, every Sutherland girl is viewed through glasses which portray her as marrying young and having children as a means of living a good life.

This rule or image is transmitted from generation to generation both by example and through ongoing interactions with family members. The Sutherland woman who rejects such an image may lose her place in the family or, at the least, encounter harsh criticism.

Our churches and our patriarchal society further contribute to such a role-limited mosaic of a woman by projecting images upon her that present her as dependent, selfless, reactive, emotional, unentitled, and basically inferior. Consequently a woman may live with depression and a gnawing emptiness, believing that no other options exist for her. It then comes as no surprise when she attempts to fill the void with food, mood-altering substances, dependent relationships, shopping, religion, and a myriad other coping mechanisms.

How can a woman shed these projected images, which alienate her from her true self? Initially she must search out God's original intention for her life. In the book of Genesis she learns that the Creator chose nothing less than the image of God as the pattern for her creation. That image, imprinted into the fabric of woman's being, is the very embodiment of health and wholeness.

With her pedigree as God's creation, woman needs to acknowledge and to nurture the unique person God created her to be. This she can do by learning to listen to herself in response to such questions as these: What are my strengths? What are my likes and dislikes? What do I enjoy doing? How do I describe myself as a person? What do I value? What are my wants and needs? What do I appreciate in a relationship?

Such listening, though foreign to many women, can also be encouraged and facilitated through participation in a support group of women committed to discovering their true selves and to living that out both in their relationships and their work.

This search need not remove a woman from her family. Rather it encourages her to locate her uniqueness there as a woman-in-God's-image while also affirming the importance of family as the laboratory for her growth and change. God chose to grow people within the family—an environment far from perfect, but one in which God saw potential for making people. Acknowledging the parts of her true self that her family has both nurtured and affirmed is as essential to the search as is discarding those images contrary to her self.

May God grant us courage to listen to the voice within, which calls us to discover and to nurture the women we were created to be.

Questions for Reflection

1. With which part of the parable did you most identify?

2. What were some of the images on the glasses in your family which became part of your mosaic?

3. Which images have been especially hard for you to overcome?

4. Describe the way your family views you today.

5. In what ways have you learned to listen to the voice within? How has that changed your understanding of yourself?

6. Write a poem, a song, a letter expressing God's attitude regarding your search for self.

Suggested Resources

Bradshaw, John. *Bradshaw On: The Family.* Deerfield Beach, Fla.: Health Communications, Inc., 1988.

Hancock, Emily. *The Girl Within.* New York: Ballantine Books, 1989.

Zdenek, Marilee. *Splinters in My Pride.* Waco, Tex.: Word Books, 1979.

7

Women and Their Self-Esteem
Helen Havlik

*W*hen a woman believes that she is equal, she is called uppity. When we stand up for what we know and what we believe, we are called aggressive and unfeminine. When we state that women are wonderful and that we are proud to be a woman, we are told that we are anti-male. When we put forth our perceptions, we are told that we don't understand reality. When we put forth our values, we are told that we are crazy and we just don't understand the way the world works. Is it any wonder that we sometimes have trouble with self-esteem?

Anne Wilson Shaef

*A*s I sit to write this chapter on self-esteem, I am beset by self-doubt. I worry that I am certainly not the best person to write this. I cannot tell anyone how to have more self-esteem. I cannot even tell myself how to have more self-esteem. Defining it is easy; doing the work, as they say in therapy circles, is not.

At least I can claim great experience with lack of self-esteem. Not too long ago, my mother asked me what it was that they as my parents had done that was so wrong (to make me so angry with them).

In a rare burst of honesty, among other things, I replied, "It would have been nice for you to teach me how to like myself."

Since then I have become aware that my parents—especially my mother—could not teach me what they did not know themselves. Low self-esteem is hereditary (if not genetic). Children learn what children see—and the first seeing and learning is in our families. If our parents have had little experience of self-love and confidence, then they are unlikely to be able to teach their children these things. In my family, this was compounded by external forces—the neighbors—who had strong ideas about what the ideal child was like. Quiet, obedient, well-behaved, never sassy.

Does any of this sound familiar? As Christians, we are reared in the faith to be meek, humble, and submissive. And especially obedient. What no one tells us is that for Christ to humble himself, he had to have a self to humble.

It is all too true that the church is one institution that does not help us or our families to develop much self-esteem. I remember going through confirmation class.

We were assigned to write a prayer. I don't remember the exact words, but they had to do with telling God how sorry I was that I was such a horrible person.

Later I told my mother about the prayer, and she was horrified. "That isn't true," she said. "You don't hate yourself."

But it was true—I thought that was what my family believed and what my church expected me to believe. My private and public lives collided, so to speak, and I was the casualty twisted in the middle.

In *Women and Self-Esteem: Understanding and Improving the Way We Think and Feel About Ourselves*, the authors state up-front what questions have led them to write.

> This book is about the millions of women whose lives and happiness have been constricted because of lack of self-esteem. How and why have so many women come to see themselves as less able, less bright, less valuable than they really are? What effects does lack of self-esteem have on individual women's psychological health, relationships, work performance, and attitudes toward others and the world in general? What effects does low self-esteem among large numbers of women have on women as a group, politically, economically, and socially?[1]

In their study, the authors cover an exhaustive range of topics I can mention only briefly here. They identify some of the common problems *women* have with self-esteem. (The point is not that men do not have problems with self-esteem. But a basic assumption of the authors is that in a patriarchal society, it is in the best interests of the dominant group—men—to keep others—such as women—down. Men do not have the same pressures placed on them that women do—we have to accept that and get over it if we ever want anything to change.)

Briefly, the six self-esteem problems are these:

1. Women tend not to know themselves well and so have no "self" to value.

2. Women may have a rigid, constrained idea of who they are because of the pressure to conform with stereotypes. Thus they may succeed in some way but still have low self-esteem.

3. Many women see themselves as complete failures and focus only on what they see as negative attributes.

4. Going one step farther, many women can see their positive traits but do not believe that they balance out their flaws.

5. Women can suffer from low self-esteem when circumstances, such as illness, force them to review their identity.

6. Women can go through periods of transition that challenge them to compare their ideal selves with current images and conclude they do not measure up.[2]

Why does this happen? Why do we get trapped in circumstances that can cause us such misery? I already have mentioned two areas that have a great impact on self-esteem—family and public life. These can be further broken down. When we talk about family it can mean our families of origin or our chosen intimates.

Many of us deal with legacies left from dysfunctional families. And often we have bought into denial so heavily that we are unaware just how troubled our families were and are. It bears repeating that parents, spouses, and other family members with self-esteem problems are bound to pass on behavior and thought-patterns that will negatively affect us sooner or later.

Public life also has a great effect on how we feel about ourselves. The institutions we deal with daily (and from a very young age) help shape how we feel about ourselves. In addition to the church, school, work, technology, government, and medicine can negatively affect us. Or think how it feels to walk down the street and be harassed by teenaged boys or construction workers.

Home is not just the house where we live, but the world we occupy. The messages the world often sends us are short on positive images. Or if the images are positive, we are often asked to compare ourselves with an impossible ideal. Can we win for losing? Low self-esteem costs us. It robs us of our creativity, our ability to take care of ourselves, our true spirituality, and so much more.

In a world that cries out for justice, the argument can be made that women with self-esteem could be a powerful source of change. The courage to take such steps as we need to help us reach our potentials—and in turn, to help others do so—is within us. Each of us is a survivor in this world. And that knowledge alone can lead to other knowledge that can lead to the sense of self that Christ had. He knew who he was and apologized to no one for it.

If we as women desire to be whole, we would do well to remember that God created and treasures us. Surely, if we are made in the image of God, we are called to celebrate ourselves, body, soul, mind, and heart, with gratitude to the one who created such amazing creatures as ourselves.

Questions for Reflections

1. What level of self-esteem do you have right now? Rank it on a scale of one to ten. What or who do you think influences your self-opinion the most? Can you remember times you were really low? Can you remember times you were on top of the world? What makes you really happy with yourself? Is it based on someone else's expectations?

2. What was your family like? Were they affirming or not? Did you learn to see yourself a certain way? Would it be wrong or disloyal to challenge that image—or are you happy with it?

3. What has your public experience been like? What things do you do well? Where do you feel the best about yourself? What experiences have affected the way you view yourself?

4. Do you identify with any of the above-mentioned self-esteem problems? Which? Are you stuck or do you see ways to change your thinking?

5. Theologically, how do you see yourself as God's creation? What Scriptures speak directly to your self-esteem? Is it possible to love your self and still be a Christian? How do you think God sees you right now?

6. The authors of *Women and Self-Esteem* suggest an exercise to help change negative thought patterns, called "Thought-Stopping."

Enlist another person to help you with this exercise. You are to sit back in a chair, get very comfortable, and close your eyes. Your friend will read the following instructions and lead you in the exercise. *You* do *not* read the exercise beyond this point; what follows are instructions for your friend.

Tell your friend to think her negative thought—whatever comes into her mind. Tell her to really get into it, to think very hard about it until she really feels terrible about herself. When you [know this has happened], pick up a book and slam it down on a table as hard as you can . . . [yelling] "STOP."[3]

At this point, the person probably has been completely startled out of the negative thought. After a little practice, we can do this for ourselves—at the onset of negativism, we can stop ourselves, replacing the negative with a positive. Sound silly? Maybe it is, but it proves that we can control what we think about ourselves—if we are willing to work at it.

7. Try affirmations. An affirmation is something about yourself that is positive and can be worded "I am. . . ." For example, if you are having trouble writing a paper, try repeating "I am a good writer" many times. Most of us are probably better at saying, "I'll never get this paper done—I'm so stupid—I can't write anything worth reading. . . ."

8. If you are dealing with self-esteem issues, do buy *Women and Self-Esteem*. It not only diagnoses the problem, it gives more suggestions on how to break out of the negative thought-patterns and judgments that keep us down. It doesn't promise miracles, but it does give realistic ideas about what is possible.

9. Consider having a group session in which you do nothing but affirm each other!

Suggested Resources

Osborne, Cecil G. *Self Esteem: Overcoming Inferiority Feelings*.

Nashville: Abingdon Press, 1986.

Ray, Veronica. *A Moment to Reflect: Meditations on Self-Esteem.* San Francisco: Harper/Hazelden, 1991.

Sanford, Linda Tschirhart and Donovan, Mary Ellen. *Women and Self-Esteem: Understanding and Improving the Way We Think and Feel About Ourselves.* New York: Penguin Books, 1985.

Schaef, Anne Wilson. *Meditations for Women Who Do Too Much.* San Francisco: Harper & Row, 1990.

8

Women and Their Body Image
Nora O. Lozano-Díaz

"Woman . . . is even required by society to make herself an erotic object. The purpose of the fashions to which she is enslaved is not to reveal her as an independent individual, but rather to cut her off from her transcendence in order to offer her as prey to male desires; thus society is not seeking to further her projects but to thwart them. The skirt is less convenient than trousers, high-heeled shoes impede walking; the least practical of gowns and dress shoes, the most fragile of hats and stocking, are most elegant; the costume may disguise the body, deform it, or follow its curves; in any case it puts it on display."

Simone de Beauvoir

Our bodies are on display for the eyes observing us. Eyes (male and female) noticing whether we have lost weight or if we have gained a little bit more. Eyes that become oppressive vigilantes, condemning us for a little hair on our chin or the shadow of a mustache. Observing eyes that seem to ask us, Have you shaved your legs? What about your underarms? Are you wearing the right dress? Did you put on just the right amount of makeup? Have you painted your nails? What about your hair? Eyes that force us to be dependent on diets, makeup, clothing that become our tyrants.

Furthermore, these vigilante eyes make statements that we internalize and then believe with all our hearts. "You are too thin!" "You are too fat!" "Your hair is not in style, it is too kinky or too straight!" "If you could just have bigger breasts!" "If you had a smaller butt!"

Women listen to these messages that tell us that we do not have the right shape, style, or balance, or that we will never achieve the longed-for approval. Meanwhile, it is interesting to observe, the eyes are considerate of men. It is acceptable for a man to have or not have hair on his legs and arms. Men can be handsome with straight, kinky, gray, white, or black hair—or no hair at all. They may be a little bit fat or thin, but it does not matter as long as they feel healthy. They look fine with or without facial hair. And they are blessed with not having to wear high-heels at all. Clearly there is something unequal about the way men's and women's bodies are viewed by our society.

Why do we succumb to the ways society tyrannizes women? Do we seek to display society's standards of beauty to gain approval and acceptance?

From childhood on, we learn that we need to play the games of society to be accepted. Many times our own mothers and aunts teach us society's rules. They do it because that is the way they too have been taught a real woman should act. My mother made me believe, probably because she also was made to believe, that women with hair under their arms smell bad. One of my aunts used to tell me, "Nora, a real woman has to have makeup on every single day, twenty-four hours a day."

Women's need for approval makes us define ourselves according to someone else's patterns. We forget or overlook who we really are. An example of this is our lack of freedom to dress as we see fit. Women who do not dress properly are the target of many critics. If we dress conservatively we are believed to be inhibited, cool, distant, even frigid. If we dress more freely, we are judged careless, indiscreet, audacious, provocative. So we put ourselves on display by using the right dress and playing the game.

The bottom line for many women is the need for approval from one man. We submit ourselves to society's demands and become people pleasers because we are afraid of being left alone. We are terrified of all the connotations that the words "single" or "unwed" convey in a world where women escorted by men seem more welcome.

Not all women can fit the standards that society has given us about what it is to be "a woman." Some women may not even be interested in fulfilling the criteria for perfect womanhood. But even though not all women can or want to be slim, tan, delicate, tall, or ideal like models, most women feel the pressure or unsatisfied desire to be perfect. Unfortunately, this pressure many times goes against our own bodies. Since many of us are not the "perfect" woman but are instead short, fat, hairy, endowed with big hips or abundant breasts, we become insecure about our bodies.

When does all this begin? When do women start having problems with body image? I think the problem starts when we are little girls, and it develops throughout our lives unless we intentionally stop it. As girls we begin forming our self-esteem, low or high, depending on the messages we hear about our bodies. Two of my best friends wear the same size clothing. One complains a good deal about her figure; the other friend thinks that she is an attractive woman.

After hearing their stories, we found that the difference between them is that the one who complains heard many bad comments about her body when she was a little girl. But the other one grew up hearing positive comments about how good-looking and beautiful she was. These early remarks about their bodies made the difference between how each perceives herself even now.

Messages about our bodies may have come from our immediate and extended family, friends, schoolteachers and classmates, church people, or the mass media. Many times we received mixed messages from these different sources. For instance, the church would tell us, "The body is not important, in fact women's bodies are bad and dirty. The soul is what we should care for." Meanwhile the media would affirm, "Your body is everything; through your body, if you have the right shape, you can get what you want and need."

But certainly the most important messages are those

we received at home. Years later our body image remains influenced by those messages, as well as those we continue receiving from the sources mentioned above and from our partners. The negative messages make us depend on the tyrants—makeup, diets, dresses, jewels, depilatories. The positive messages, however, free us to be ourselves.

The body image that the messages shape affect all areas of our lives. A woman with a good body image looks and feels more comfortable whatever she does, regardless of whether she obeys the demands of the tyrants or not. This ease contrasts with the imprisonment of the woman who depends on external factors to be happy, beautiful, or secure—and thus will never have enough. Outside factors never provide us with the security and power to accept and live with our selves as we truly are.

This is not to say that makeup, diets, exercise, and so forth are completely bad or that we should avoid them entirely. I like to walk for exercise. I like to go shopping and discover new stores. The problem comes when we depend on all these things to be happy, secure, or whole. When the lack of a new dress, right makeup, or an expensive perfume makes us feel anxious and insecure, it is time to review our self-esteem. It is time to examine where our self-worth resides and what is stopping us from accepting ourselves the way that we are.

The gift of acceptance and love for ourselves comes from the inside. That is why we have to explore our own true selves to find who we really are. Perhaps we will find many hurts from negative messages that we have received, but facing them is the first step to the process of healing.

If we continue to be on display, hiding behind the demands of the tyrants, we will spend our time, money, and energy on external factors that will not help us to feel better in the long run. We must instead work on who we are, what we want, where we are going, what is healthy for us and what is not. It is time to start defining our true selves according to our own standards. We need to be subjects of our lives instead of objects of someone else's life.

Certainly, this is not easy work, and we will face much pressure to return to the old patterns. One way we counteract the pressure is to nurture a circle of supporters who share our values. Their commitment to values different than society's helps shield us from society's voices long enough to hear our own.

In dealing with my own problem of body image, several things have helped me.

1. I recognize that I am made in the image of God. God formed me carefully with God's own hands (Ps. 139:13-16). I am not an accident of nature!

2. I recognize that body image and self-esteem are common problems for everybody. The only difference is that for some people the problem is bigger and for others smaller. Sometimes I meet women who do not seem to have any problem of body image at all, and I feel intimidated. When that happens I try to talk to that "perfect" woman. As I get close to her, I soon find that she is struggling or she has struggled with the same issues that I have.

3. If I am able to remember a specific experience when a negative comment was made about myself, I go back to that moment and try to understand why and how

that comment was made. Was it said because of me? Or was it a reflection of the other person's problems or needs?

4. I talk to the people closest to me, especially my partner, about how their careless or negative messages about my body do psychological and emotional violence to my self-esteem. Many times they make statements without realizing their harm. The best solution is to risk naming these issues and explaining how I feel when such comments are made.

5. I look at myself with the same mercy that I offer other women or people in general. If I see a heavy woman, I usually think for a second that she is heavy. Then I automatically concentrate on her interior qualities—she is smart, fun, or compassionate. Most of the time I do not judge a person by physical appearance. This helps me feel that generally I am not judged by my body, but by who I am internally.

6. I am being thankful for what I have, instead of complaining about the things that I do not have. I will never forget an experience I had several years ago with one of my dear grandmothers, who has been in a wheelchair for over a decade.

One day we were watching TV together. During a commercial I made a comment about how the woman in the ad did not have pretty legs. My grandmother replied, "Nora, that does not matter, they work."

Questions for Reflection

1. What messages did you hear about your body when little from your family, classmates, church, or society in general?

2. What are your reasons for obeying many of the "tyrants" (makeup, shaving, waxing, fashion) of this society?

3. What are your standards for feeling secure about your body image? Are you happy with them? Would you like to change them? If so, what would you like your new standards to be?

4. Is there something that you need to tell to the people closest to you regarding the comments they make about your body?

5. Reflect on the image of God forming your own body. Give thanks for your own uniqueness in God's creation.

Suggested Resources

Boston Women's Health Book Collective. *The New Our Bodies, Our Selves*. New York: Simon and Schuster, 1991.

Congo, Janet. *Finding Inner Security*. California: Regal Books, 1985.

Freedman, Rita. *Bodylove*. New York: Harper & Row, 1988.

Hutchinson, Marcia. *Transforming Body Image*. Trumansberg, N.Y.: Crossing Press, 1985.

Wilson Schaef, Anne. *Women's Reality*. Minnesota: Winston Press, 1981.

9

Women and Their Sexuality
Carol M. Schreck

*T*he lack of knowledge the woman has about her body and about what gives her pleasure and the lack of responsibility for her erotic satisfaction are ancient legacies of an attitude toward the female body which regards it as fundamentally asexual, an instrument through which the man enjoys himself and the babies are born. A woman has a responsibility to her body, not only to take care of its procreative potential, but to own its inherent possibilities for giving and receiving pleasure.

Penelope Washbourn

*T*he ancient legacy of asexuality which contemporary women still carry was influenced by the mind-body dualism characteristic of Greek culture during the early Christian era. The Greeks believed the mind/spirit was imprisoned in the body. Only through denial of the body could one achieve ultimate truth.

This dualist mind-set significantly affected Christian thoughts and attitudes, including those about women. They were viewed as emotional, nonthinking, and therefore concerned primarily with issues pertaining to the lesser reality—the body. As a result, women—and their reality—were seen as inferior.

A similar disparagement of women, though for different reasons, is found in the patriarchal legacy of the Old Testament. Here women were regarded as property to be secured and disposed of by the man. A woman was considered part of a man's assets, numbered along with his offspring, servants, and cattle. The inferior place this gave to women is reflected in the recitation a Hebrew female would have heard on the lips of many a devout male when he recited the common Talmudic prayer,

> Blessed art thou who didst not make me a Gentile
> Blessed art thou who didst not make me a *woman*
> Blessed art thou who didst not make me a boar.[1]

Not surprisingly, Hebrew cultic rules prohibited women from reading or studying Torah. Should a woman touch Torah, it had to be burned to be kept pure. When a woman menstruated, she was considered *niddah* (or defiled) and was required to isolate herself from others to avoid contaminating them. Perhaps this accounts for the fact that even today women sometimes refer to their monthly menstruation as "the curse."[2]

These devastating legacies, however, stand in sharp contrast to an alternative view of femaleness grounded both in the biblical account of creation and in the record of Jesus' interaction with women. Both of these scriptural sources had long been disregarded and peripheralized in the tradition of the church, in favor of the dualistic and patriarchal themes. Yet they are now providing the impetus for a new understanding by women of their need to reclaim and reaffirm the uniqueness and goodness of that which is female.

Christian women no longer are content to be relegated to second-class status, as objects to be used and abused by men. Instead women are embarking on a journey of rediscovering the full meaning of the biblical assertion that woman also—and not only man—was created in the image of God.

An essential part of this journey is for women to gain a well-developed understanding of their sexuality. It is helpful to conceive of sexuality as having three components. The first has to do with gender (in this case, being female). The second deals with sex roles (the societal or cultural notion of "feminine behavior"). The third is concerned with erotic potential (what is sexually stimulating).

The challenge before Christian women is to have their understanding of each of these aspects of sexuality be biblically informed. Included in that challenge is the whole matter of women assuming responsibility for the implications of their sexuality.

For women the issue of gender, understood from a biblical perspective, means nothing less than recognizing the inherent goodness of being female. Women are created in the image of God—and bear the image of God—in their physical bodies. Thus every woman must embrace her gender-specific body as crucial to her self-formation.

It is essential that a woman see her genitalia as an integral part of her divinely intended creaturehood, not as a concession or a postscript on God's part to an otherwise already established identity. Therefore, knowing her body intimately, and experiencing her body without shame, are both aspects of a genuine acceptance of the gender dimension of sexuality based in creation theology.

Since the issue of women's sex roles was addressed in previous chapters, it will not be considered here, except to make one connection with the biblical creation account. Genesis 1 addresses gender by unequivocally applying "image of God" to female and male alike. But it also seems to address sex roles by indicating that the mandate to "be fruitful and multiply, and fill the earth and subdue it" is given to male and female alike. Women's sex roles thus include options as limitless as God's creative ability. Women are called to be co-creators with Creator God.

This challenge is aptly captured by the title Elizabeth O'Connor gave to her book about creativity and gifts: *Eighth Day of Creation.*[3] After God's creative working and resting during the seven days of the creation story, the creative work is continued. However, in this "eighth day," women and men are called on to create, to express their sexuality through creating, tending, and nurturing life.

In addition, sexuality pertains to God in that God gifted human beings with erotic potential. In other words, God has bestowed on women the ability to expe-

rience sexual gratification through their senses. Therefore, it is a woman's right, as well as her responsibility, to
explore her body to discover what is stimulating to her
and what parts of her body, when touched, sexually
arouse, stimulate, and satisfy her.

Such self-knowledge also is beneficial for healthy
functioning in a sexual relationship with a trusted other.
When a woman knows her body she can assume responsibility for communicating her sexual needs to her partner.

Body awareness allows a woman to define what is
important to her sexual intimacy needs while at the same
time discouraging any tendency to espouse the male definition of sexuality and pleasure. Inclinations on the part
of women to adopt the male standard for sexual arousal
distort the uniqueness of female sexuality and ignore the
complementarity of woman and man.

In summary, for women to affirm themselves sexually is to choose to participate in life as sexual beings and
to share themselves as such with others. Sexuality is a
good gift from God to and for women; it is an integral
part of women's wholeness.

For women to ignore their sexuality is tantamount
to saying to God, "You didn't mean it, it's not important."
The biblical record, however, indicates that sexuality is
an important part of what God intended in creating
women in the divine image. Thus sexuality remains both
a gift and a responsibility as women discover what it
means to be female and to nurture the sexual complementarity with which they are entrusted.

Questions for Reflection

1. What were the early messages that were part of your legacy regarding your sexuality? List them under the three categories discussed in this article—gender, roles, and erotic pleasure.

2. In what areas have you succeeded in overcoming the negative messages about your sexuality. How have you done this?

3. Describe the day you started to menstruate. Include your thoughts and feelings as you approached this passage of becoming a woman.

4. What do you experience as being sexually erotic?

5. Give thanks to God for the gift of your sexuality.

Suggested Resources

Heiman, J. and LoPiccolo, L. and J. *Becoming Orgasmic: A Sexual Growth Program for Women*. Englewood Cliffs, New Jersey: Prentice-Hall, Inc., 1976.

Kaplan, Helen Singer. *Disorders of Sexual Desire*. New York: Brunner/Mazel, 1979.

Louden, Jennifer. "Self-Pleasuring," *The Woman's Comfort Book*. New York: Harper Collins Publishers, 1992.

Washbourn, Penelope. *Becoming Woman*. San Francisco: Harper & Row, 1977.

10

Women and Intimacy
Elouise Renich Fraser

*T*rue intimacy with another human being can only be experienced when you have
found true peace within yourself.

Angela L. Wozniak

Kindness and intelligence don't always deliver
us from the pitfalls and traps. There is no way to
take the danger out of human relationships.

Barbara Grizzuti Harrison

*I*ntimacy isn't an adrenaline rush or the energy
of sexual attraction. It isn't the excitement of a new relationship or the discovery of shared experiences. It isn't
the thrill of mutual risk-taking or a feeling of intense
closeness. It isn't the surge of power that possesses or the
exquisite death of being possessed.

Intimacy isn't escape into a fantasy world in which we deny our true identities. It isn't absorption of one person's thoughts, feelings, and desires into those of the other. It isn't bonding against a common enemy, or preoccupation with telling and retelling our victim stories. Nor is it the "perfect" reciprocal relationship in which all my needs are met by you, and you never make a request I cannot fulfill.

It's easy to settle for pseudo-intimacy. It looks and feels great. It doesn't seem at first to be very demanding. In fact, it often feels natural, even "meant to be." It can give a kind of order to our lives, a sense of direction, a reason to get up in the morning, a profound sense of being known and understood.

There's just one problem. Pseudo-intimacy doesn't bring people closer together. It creates fog. It distances us from reality and makes us strangers. Not just to ourselves, but to each other and to the fullness of life itself. Close bodies don't make close friends.

I long for true intimacy in my relationships. I've tasted it, and I want more. But I also fear it. Intimacy doesn't just happen. It comes to people who have chosen to work hard—not so much on their relationships, as on *themselves.*

Even though I've known intimacy, I feel like a beginner. Not just in new relationships, in which I always go through the awkwardness of finding my way, but in old relationships. Neither of us knows what's around the next corner. It's difficult to let go of the illusion that past intimacy makes me an expert on the present.

I've found encouragement and empowerment in several places—in conversations with other women and men, daily meditation books, self-help books on women's relationships, and most recently in a booklet by Marilyn Mason.[1] Here are some things I've found helpful.

First, intimacy isn't a possession. It's a quality of relationship which emerges freely and grows over time between two people or within a group. No one owes me intimacy. I am not in charge of making it happen. I cannot plan for it, orchestrate it, or hang onto it. It comes and it goes. It isn't something I learn to do, then take with me from one relationship or group to another.

Nor is intimacy something another person can impose upon me. I am not obligated to become intimate with any particular person or group. The command to love one another is not a command to become intimate with everyone I meet, or even with those who would like to become intimate with me. Even though I'm not in control of making intimacy happen, I can choose *not* to let it happen.

Second, there are things I can do to become a more likely candidate for intimate relationships.[2]

I can work on *boundaries*, on where I stop and the other person begins. What belongs to me, and what belongs to you. The difference between my feelings and your feelings. Where my responsibility ends and yours begins. What is my business and what is none of my business. How much time and energy I have and don't have. How to give myself without giving myself away.

I can work on *self-esteem*. Do I like myself? Do I even know myself? Am I willing to let go of my preoccupation with what other people are thinking, feeling, and doing, so I can get clear on what *I* am thinking, feeling, and doing? Are my choices based on what is good for *me*? Am I willing to put energy into things that matter to *me*? Do I truly believe that what is good for me is good for the people around me?

I can learn to *trust*. Give up my knee-jerk, people-pleasing "of-course-I-trust-you" reaction and discover that I have choices. Not everyone asking for my trust is trustworthy. Actions speak louder than words. I can't always guarantee that I won't be hurt, even when I've made carefully considered choices.

I can become *self-aware*. Aware of my patterns of denial. Aware of ways in which my words and actions are at odds with each other. Aware of what I'm looking for and am willing to give in relationships. I can take steps in response to this self-awareness, and gain even greater self-awareness in the backlash from within and without.

I can learn to be *assertive*, to ask for what I need and want. To disclose my thoughts and feelings. To be willing to listen to whatever response I get. To decide how I feel about it. And then to consider my options. I can begin letting go of passivity that invites victimization and aggression that insists on doing it my way.

Third, the mystery of intimacy isn't destroyed by talking about it. Indeed it may be multiplied. There are hundreds of ways to express closeness and connectedness, and many settings in which this can happen. Most of us have tunnel vision. Talking it over with each other, and finding out when intimacy happens to other people, can open our eyes. Maybe there's more intimacy in my life than I've yet learned to recognize or appreciate.

Fourth, we all have rules for avoiding intimacy. Stay busy. Talk about the weather. Don't express unpleasant emotions, such as anger or disappointment, especially if they're feelings I have toward you. Make jokes all the time. Never question patterns of relating that don't feel comfortable for me, especially if the other person seems happy with them. Don't look the other person in the eye. Change the subject if I feel uncomfortable. And be sure to fill every silence. If I'm going to open myself to the possibility of intimacy, I'm going to have to break some rules.

Fifth, my capacity for intimacy is directly related to my willingness to keep the focus on myself. Sometimes I feel let down. I don't experience the closeness and connectedness I wanted or expected. Or I begin to realize there's more pseudo-intimacy in one or two of my friendships than I'm comfortable with any longer. It's easy to waste time and emotional energy trying to analyze my friends. If they would just work harder on *their* boundaries, low self-esteem, trust issues, need for self-awareness, and passivity/aggression, we could enjoy much more intimacy. No doubt. But would *I* be ready?

Ironically, the nature of intimacy demands that I let go of the other person's readiness for intimacy, and concentrate on my own. Am I willing to risk sharing with another human being some of the things I've been working on in *myself?* Am I willing to break some of *my* rules for avoiding intimacy? Am I willing to make choices and take actions that reveal *my* true thoughts and feelings?

When the student is willing, the gift will appear.

Questions for Reflection

1. What are your personal rules for avoiding intimacy? If you get stuck, just think about your family-of-origin dynamics!

2. Does your group have rules for avoiding intimacy? What are they?

3. How many kinds of intimacy can you name and describe? Which are most familiar or comfortable for you? Do you know which kinds of intimacy your closest friends prefer?

4. I mentioned five areas for personal growth: boundaries, self-esteem, trust, self-awareness, and assertiveness. Can you think of other things women can work on to become more likely candidates for intimate relationships? What one or two things stand out as issues for you?

Suggested Resources

Davis Kasl, Charlotte. *Women, Sex, and Addiction: A Search for Love and Power.* New York: Harper & Row, 1989.

Goldhor Lerner, Harriet. *The Dance of Intimacy: A Woman's Guide to Courageous Acts of Change in Key Relationships.* New York: Harper & Row, 1989.

Mason, Marilyn. "Intimacy," Hazeldon Foundation, 1986.

Pennbaker, James W. *Opening Up: The Healing Power of Confiding in Others.* New York: Avon Books, 1990.

Thoele, Sue Patton. *The Courage to Be Yourself: A Woman's Guide to Growing Beyond Emotional Dependence.* Berkeley, Calif.: Conari Press, 1991.

11

Women and Their Anger
Elouise Renich Fraser

> *B*ecause society would rather we always wore a pretty face, women have been trained to cut off anger.
>
> *Nancy Friday*

> Anger repressed can poison a relationship as surely as the cruelest words.
>
> *Joyce Brothers*

*I*n my family anger was a deadly sin. Something to be suppressed or gotten rid of as quickly and quietly as possible. Sort of like swallowing a piece of liver in one lump sum. You gagged, but you knew it was good for you.

For most of my life, I haven't had clear ways of thinking about anger. Now that I'm an adult, I often get into trouble when I talk about anger. It doesn't seem to make much difference what I say or how I say it. It's always too much or too loud. Too soon or too one-sided.

The subject matter itself generates high anxiety. I used to think this was because Christians believe anger is a sin. Now I'm not so sure. Maybe it's because there isn't a human being alive who hasn't been deeply scarred by someone else's anger, or agonized over angry words they've turned loose on a friend or family member. Words spoken in anger quickly take on a life of their own. We don't like being reminded of their power to destroy.

It's impossible to talk about anger as though it were a general concept. Anger doesn't exist somewhere out there, floating anonymously in the air, waiting for me to decide what to do with it. I know only the anger that comes to me from other people and my own anger as it wells up within me.

Like everything else in my life, anger has a context. It's always connected to what I'm doing or not doing, saying or not saying, signaling or not signaling right now. Anger isn't an outside, impersonal force that invades my world at will. It's an emotional response to a particular situation—past, present, or projected into the future.

Although anger isn't a deadly sin, it can be deadly in its effects. When anger is directed toward me, survival techniques are in order. Here are some that work for me.

Silence. Most angry outbursts require no response from me at all. This is hard to accept. My gut instinct has always been to defend myself. But defending myself buys into the other person's harsh judgment of me and signals my willingness to accept shame or blame. Letting go of the need to fight back may be as simple as holding my tongue.

Distancing. If anger is abusive, I can run. For my life, if necessary. More often, for my emotional well-being. Is this cowardly? Rude? Refusal to take the other person seriously? Not necessarily. It may be a graphic way of taking that person with the greatest possible seriousness. He or she is as entitled to anger as I am, even though the anger may be misdirected. Distancing myself may also be a courageous way to stay in touch with my own feelings and sense of dignity. Exercising this option may be as simple (or as difficult!) as calmly leaving the room. Without stomping my feet, slamming the door, or trying to get in a so-called last word.

Staying out of the way. I have a habit of setting myself up for indirect, passive-aggressive anger. Especially from men, but also from family members. No angry outbursts here! Just patterns of "forgetting," half-completed tasks, clutter around the house, lateness, carelessness, hair in the sink and on the soap, and a thousand other mundane annoyances. All of them guaranteed to make me angry. The irony is that *I* end up looking and sounding like the villain, even though these behaviors are expressions of someone else's anger toward me.

Staying out of the way means that I choose not to react angrily to these situations. I choose instead to leave the unexpressed anger where it belongs—right in the other person's gut! This is hard. It means learning to believe the other person's repeated actions, instead of his or her repeated promises to do better next time. It means giving up my chosen role as The Enforcer. And it means getting on with *my* business.

Keeping an open mind. Even angry outbursts may contain truth about me. Not the truth about my worth as a woman. And not necessarily the truth about my behavior or my inner motives. Yet sometimes angry outbursts seem to hit the nail on the head. They contain things that are "true" about me. But I am never under obligation to answer the harsh judges of this world. I am free. Free to refuse to be drawn into this person's inventory of my faults and weaknesses.

I'm also free to reflect on the situation. Perhaps I sparked the attack with an unkind word. A critical attitude. Or a hidden desire for revenge. Keeping an open mind doesn't mean standing by, ready to accept responsibility for someone else's anger. It just means inquiring into *my* side of the relationship, and attending to anything that is *my* business. If I've taken care of my own business, that's the most I can do. God alone is my judge.

Then there's my own anger. I'm learning to survive this, too. Here are several strategies I find helpful.

Self-examination. Inevitably, anger distorts the way I perceive reality. I may think I know exactly whom I'm angry with, and why. But what's *really* going on here?

A quick check sometimes reveals a deeper truth. My anger may be fueled by unfinished family business into which this other person has unknowingly stumbled. It may be a cover for my fear or pain—such as the fear of abandonment or the pain of having been exposed in some way. Or, it may be that I'm really angry at *myself* for getting into this situation.

Recognizing these deeper truths can help set the other person free. It can defuse some of my anger, and help me focus on the more basic issues.

Being good to myself. Like grief, anger needs to be expressed, but not indiscriminately. Not every place is a safe place. And not every person is a good listener. I owe it to myself to have some safe places and safe friends who will hear me out without condemning my anger or telling me what to do.

When I'm angry at other people, my first impulse is to react in ways that will take care of *them*, fix *them*, show *them* a thing or two! What I need for myself is a refuge. A place where I can listen to my own words, get some clues about what's going on in me, and come up with creative options for change. Not primarily for their sakes but for mine!

Keeping short accounts. Life is filled with disappointments. Small disappointments, unexpressed and collected over time, turn me into a pressure cooker. I don't like telling people I'm disappointed when plans fall through or when they don't keep an agreement with me. My people-pleasing instinct wants to smooth things over. "Oh, that's all right. Don't worry about it. It doesn't matter that much." Sometimes it doesn't. But many times it does.

It helps to express my disappointments as soon as possible, not because I want people to feel guilty, but because I need to make my true feelings known. Not just because they're important, but because I don't want them to become monstrosities. I need to express my anger. But I'm learning there are other negative feelings I also have and need to express. Carefully letting these out as they arise seems to prevent some of my pent-up, explosive anger.

Trusting the process. Whenever I express anger directly to a friend, my heart skips a beat. Time seems to stand still. And I have to remember to keep breathing. I grew up believing anger meant death. The death of the relationship.

There's truth in this. Expressing anger directly *does* often feel like the end. But maybe it's a good end. Maybe it's time for change and growth. Perhaps my anger is a clue to an injustice that's being overlooked. A sign that I care deeply about the relationship. Or an indication that I trust my friend enough to risk inviting his or her response.

Questions for Reflection

1. What were your family rules about anger?

2. Do you remember seeing your parents or other caretakers angry at each other? What lessons did you learn from their modeling?

3. Must anger always be expressed directly and verbally? If not, can you give a clear example of how you might let your anger guide you into a non-angry response that doesn't sidestep what made you angry in the first place?

4. When was the last time you expressed anger directly to a friend or family member? What was it like? And when was the last time someone expressed anger directly toward you? What was that like? What has been the outcome in each case?

5. What personal strategies work for you in dealing with anger—someone else's anger toward you, and your own anger toward someone else?

Suggested Resources

Burns, David. *Feeling Good: The New Mood Therapy*. New York: New American Library, 1980.

Davis Kasl, Charlotte. *Women, Sex, and Addiction: A Search for Love and Power*. New York: Harper & Row, 1989.

Goldhor Lerner, Harriet. *The Dance of Anger: A Woman's Guide to Changing the Patterns of Intimate Relationships*. New York: Harper & Row, 1985.

Harrison, Beverly Wildung. "The Power of Anger in the Work of Love," Beverly Wildung Harrison and Carol S. Robb, eds. *Making the Connections*. Boston: Beacon Press, 1985.

12

Women and
Their Friendships
Anne Baxter

"I'd say women do not have close relationships with other women. Female solidarity, as far as I can tell, is a lie perpetuated by the women's movement."[1]

*F*or centuries women have been bonding together, drawing strength and comfort from each other during the struggles of life. Our great-grandmothers congregated to cook for barn-raisings and church picnics, chatted over quilting bees, gathered in each others kitchens for comfort. A Native American tribal custom set a lodge up in the community where women remained together while menstruating.

Knowledge about breast-feeding and herbal remedies have been passed along orally from mother, midwife, neighbor to young women. One of my favorite biblical passages portrays Mary, after learning she was pregnant, running to Elizabeth for support and encouragement and being received with joy. Women have been sharing in each other's labor, dreams, joys, and sorrows since time began.

Now, more than ever, we need each other as women. Times have changed. The role of women in today's culture is confusing. We are bombarded by countless images, some absurd, some appealing, of what a woman should be. Now more than ever women have the freedom to sift through this multitude of images and voices and decide individually who we are, how we will live, and what we want to be about.

We can be poets or firefighters, lawyers or pastors, married mothers or single mothers. We can be angry, we can be gentle, we can be nurturing. We can be politically involved, we can be economically self-sufficient, we can be protestors.

Technology has made our lives simpler yet infinitely more complex as well. Microwaves and washing machines free our time, yet driving children to dance lessons, answering the telephone, and being committee members on church boards fill our lives with busyness. It is easy in this myriad of activity to loose touch with ourselves.

Now, more than ever, we need each other as women. We need safe places where we can draw together amidst the craziness of life to affirm who we are, to struggle with who we are becoming, to find acceptance and compassion when we simply aren't holding all the pieces together. We need friendships that are warm havens, friends to laugh with and remember with, friends to remind us that we are more than a pastor, a wife, a mother, a doctor, or a shopkeeper. There is something about a good, solid friend that is priceless.

Luise Eichenbaum and Susie Orbach have written an insightful and encouraging book on the nature of friendship between women. In *Between Women* they write about the life-giving quality of such friendships. Yet they also write with great insight about the shadow side of women's friendships—the dynamics within us *and* between us as women that can undermine the solidity of female friendships. Raising our awareness of such dynamics can help us care for the friendships with important women in our lives.

Carol Gilligan, in her hallmark book, *In a Different Voice*, explains how the traditional model of mother as primary caregiver affects boys and girls. The mother becomes the main figure against which a child creates his or her sense of self. Boys, by comparing themselves to their mothers, see that they are different. They learn that it is comfortable to be separate and distinct from people.

As girls compare themselves to their mothers, they see that they are similar. Girls learn that it is comfortable to be alike and connected to the world and other people. While each woman will have her own comfort level with both separateness and connectedness, a desire for and a comfortableness with being attached and connected are part of our psyche as women.[2]

We bring great gifts to the world and to our relationships by living as women from this point of connectedness. Our gifts include sensitivity, the ability to intuit and empathize with another, the capacity to converse at a level which reaches our core and marrow, compassion.

However, as Eichenbaum and Orbach allude to time and again in their book, the gift of connectedness which enriches our relationships can also cause tension. Along with the joy of connecting comes an underbelly of hurt—"The pain of jealousy, the pain of envy, the pain of anger, the pain of competition, the pain of abandonment, the pain of betrayal, the pain of wanting. . . ."[3]

It is easy for women to become deeply connected or enmeshed in a relationship. Enmeshment with another person occurs when we begin to blur the boundaries between ourselves and another person. When we are connecting at this level, changes that happen in the relationship or to a friend seem to threaten our sense of self or the relationship. "Almost every woman," Eichenbaum and Orbach write, "can recall at least one occasion where a friend told her of some good fortune and she was startled to discover that she felt uncomfortable."[4]

My most vivid of such recollections centers around my best friend's marriage. I was struggling through my first year of grad school, living on a frayed shoestring, when my best friend and roommate got married. She moved into a house with her new husband and continued her work as an art teacher.

I celebrated with her, yet I felt quite alone. My own life seemed shoddy and transient next to hers. While months before I had been relishing the freedom and sense of adventure and purpose that came with my decision to go to seminary, suddenly I felt young, career-less, and broke. I was also secretly afraid that our friendship would fade away now that the externals of our life were veering off into different courses.

Accustomed to our usual connectedness as friends, I was feeling threatened by the sudden separateness of our lives. I did not talk with her about these feelings for some time. For a while they affected my capacity to be close with her.

I had to learn to reaffirm the validity and beauty of my own lifestyle instead of feeling intimidated by the different identity she was creating for herself. In time, I realized that our friendship would endure the changes that occurred in our lives.

When two people are connected at a deep level and change occurs which shakes the status quo of the relationship, it is not surprising that "negative" emotions emerge which are neither desired nor understood. Instead of being happy over a friend's success, a woman may feel threatened. Because such feelings go against that unwritten law of connectedness, these feelings are often hidden away. Orbach and Eichenbaum write,

> When such painful feelings emerge in a . . . friendship they can cause havoc and distress. The intensity with which they are experienced can be almost unbearable. And yet equally unbearable (or unthinkable) is the thought of talking directly to one's friend about the upset. For within women's relationships there seems to be more fear in talking about anger or hurt than there is within a marriage.[5]

We often choose to withdraw from our friend, physically or emotionally, rather than face the issue head-on with her. Emotions not expressed, however, eat away at a friendship. Vocalized or not, they find avenues to seep out and affect the capacity for true intimacy.

A few years after my friend was married, we began talking about some of the feelings we had each experienced during the transitional years of our lives. I admitted to her that watching her change after marriage had been scary for me. It was strange to see her grow into an efficient and organized housekeeper after our previous "creative chaos," strange to see her life so stable while mine remained in the flux and transition of student life.

I admitted that sometimes I feared she was silently thinking, *My, what chaos Anne lives with, never knowing what she wants to do next, never knowing if her car will make it to work, never knowing where the rent will come from!* She confessed to me that sometimes she longs for the freedom and spontaneity that marks my life.

It was a relief to talk. We ended up realizing how deeply enriching these differences could be and how much we need the altering points of view we bring to each other's lives. The feelings that we feared, when expressed, merely deepened the connection that had existed all along.

As human beings, we want to be loved for who we are. As women, we grow up holding parts of ourselves back for fear that if we are too difficult, too stubborn, or too vocal we will be rejected. It is easy simply to repeat the tightrope walking we learned as children, trying to maintain balance between being who we are and being what we think people will like. We hide away ourselves to create false peace, and miss the chance to be known and loved for who we really are.

It is important to ask who we will entrust with this

gift of ourselves. Yet if we take the risk of being our true selves within the context of our close and trusted female friends, if we risk talking about those "shameful" emotions, we will be on the road toward finding balance between separateness and connectedness.

Now more than ever, we need each other as women. Take the risk with the women in your life. With love and gentleness, begin to speak what is truly of you. Remember, the world is waiting for the daughters of God to be revealed.

Questions for Reflection:

1. Relive the stories of your important female friendships. What feelings are connected to the memory of these friendships?

2. What patterns do you see emerging as you relive these stories?

3. How are you at balancing the need to be both separate and connected in your friendships? Where is your cutting edge?

4. How are you at dealing with such "unspeakable" emotions as anger, competition, envy in your relationships with other women? What friendships provide a safe place for you to address these issues?

5. How can you intentionally celebrate the friendships in your life, nurturing and protecting them? Looking back on friendships that have been severed, are there people you need to reconnect with for the sake of healing?

Suggested Resources

Block, Joel D. *Friendship*. New York: MacMillan Publishing Co., Inc., 1980.

Eichenbaum, Luise and Orbach, Susie. *Between Women*. New York: Viking Penguin, Inc. 1988.

Gilligan, Carol. *In a Different Voice*. Cambridge: Harvard University Press, 1982.

13

Women and Their Self-Care
Nora O. Lozano-Díaz

> *T*eacher, which commandment in the
> law is the greatest?' He said to him, 'You shall
> love the Lord your God with all your heart, and
> with all your soul, and with all your mind.' This
> is the greatest and first commandment. And a
> second is like it: 'You shall love your neighbor as
> yourself.' "
>
> *Matthew 22:36-39*

*I*t was a sunny and hot afternoon in July, the ap-
pointed day to discuss the important topic of women
taking care of themselves.[1] Carol, Elouise, Helen, Anne,
and I gathered at Carol's house, ready to share our own
ideas and feelings regarding the issue. By the end of the
afternoon, we affirmed with conviction that this task of
taking care of one's self is a must if we are to survive in

this world which demands so much from us as women.

Unfortunately, taking care of the self does not happen automatically, as breathing or digesting do. No! Taking care of the self requires intentionality, time, energy, and struggle. It is hard work, but not impossible work.

The Bible verses quoted at the beginning of this section imply that the ability to share love springs from learning to love one's self. I believe that a basic way of loving one's self is taking care of one's self. It is interesting to notice that for Jesus the commandments to love God, self, and neighbor were similar because each had to be done with all of the heart, mind, and soul.

This suggests that the vital task of self-care requires all of one's being. In other words, the best of one's energy, emotions, and intellectual abilities have to be involved in this task. Unfortunately, we have been taught by society that the "perfect" woman puts herself in second place. This means that primarily she does not take care of herself or her needs. Instead she takes care of others and their needs. For this reason, self-care is difficult for women.

Taking care of the self is a personal matter. Certainly it affects the lives of other people—but in the end the task belongs only to the one doing it. The process is one in which a woman learns to take better care first of herself then of others. This is not selfishness, nor is it taking away from others something that belongs to them. Rather, it is giving something to one's self.

In more simple words, taking care of one's self is recognizing one's needs, and doing something to fulfill them. It is self-caring. A realization of its importance often comes at those very moments when one has failed to do so. Yet at these moments, the future offers a new beginning. Learning to take care of one's self is a lifelong, hope-filled process.

The first step in this process is knowing one's self, particularly what one needs. There is no recipe that works for every woman. What works for you may not work for me. It is common for women to struggle to know who we are and what we need. Many women have been taught to be selfless and needless and that their purpose is to fulfill the needs of others.

If this is your case, start by exploring yourself and your needs. Praying and meditating, talking with other women who are facing this same issue, joining a support group, beginning therapy, journaling—all are tools you can use to get in touch with your self and your needs. Since people are continually changing, this process of self-evaluation has to be done periodically. The first time may be hard, but with practice it gets easier.

What does taking care of the self look like? As mentioned before, the task is a very personal one and depends on a woman's personality, her particular life stage, and her needs in that specific moment.

For an introverted woman, self-care may involve time to be alone and recharge her energy to continue being in relationship with the world. An extroverted woman may care for her self through spending a whole afternoon with a group of friends. A mother may hire a babysitter to gain time for and by herself. An overworked woman may take a comforting bubble bath at the end of the day.

Taking care of one's self may mean buying a new dress, getting a haircut, taking some time to pray or exercise or rest, talking to a friend, or attending a support group. It may mean giving oneself permission to have an organized life or a disorganized one, to have some routines or none at all.

Taking care of the self has a cost. One cost is a change in the way people may perceive you. They may see you as becoming selfish and irresponsible, for your time, money, and energy may not be as readily available for their use. This is especially likely if you have been overextending yourself to take care of others and their needs. You might even be accused of not living out the model of Christian servanthood.

In the process of taking care of yourself, you can expect, at least at the beginning, to feel some resentment from other people. This can be scary, causing you guilt and anguish.

However, not taking care of the self has an even greater cost. Overextension and not listening to one's needs will eventually lead to emotional, financial, spiritual, or physical burnout.

There is a cost to be paid, whether one takes care of one's self or not. The questions a woman must ask are, "Which cost is healthier in the long run? Will I continue taking care of the other people until I am empty? Or will I run the risk of facing people's resentments or labels so I can be healthy and content, both with myself and with those I love?"

If you start taking care of yourself, you will experience a pleasant surprise. Even though at the beginning the people around you may feel upset, angry, and abandoned, soon you and they will find out that this seeming abandonment is a gift. This gift consists in the discovery that they too can learn to take care of themselves. As you let them go, they will learn who they are, what their identity is, and what they need and want to take care of themselves. They may not know how to do it at the beginning, but they can learn in the same way that you are.

We must remember as women that we have choices. We can say "Yes" to a certain person, event, invitation, or request. Or we can say "No." The no is the challenge; how we want to please people and make them happy! How readily we agree to things that we do not want to do!

We need to recognize and accept our limitations and establish our priorities. Realize, therefore, that one woman cannot satisfy all the needs and expectations of those around her. Give yourself permission to say "No." This may upset some people, but they will find other avenues for meeting their needs. Remember, you are not indispensable!

Here are signs to help you recognize if you are taking care of yourself. First you need to learn to listen to your body. Symptoms such as stress, apprehension, anxious dreams, lack of sleep, uneasiness, fatigue, loneliness, anger, irritability, or impatience may be signs that you are overloaded. When you feel trapped, without choices, resentful, left out, or that life is just passing by without your active participation, most likely you are not taking care of yourself.

The tendency is to ignore these signs. But sooner or later they will come back, maybe with more force, to warn you that something is wrong and that you need to listen to yourself. Do not let this happen. As soon as one of these elements shows up, start exploring yourself to see what you need.

This task of taking care of the self has been described as hard work, time consuming, and almost impossible. But one last adjective to describe the challenge is *rewarding*. When you undertake this work you are saying, "I am important. I am worthy enough to spend these resources on fulfilling my needs. I am capable of making my own decisions."

Through such affirmations we challenge the ambiguous messages we have received as women regarding our sense of capability, worth, and self-esteem. By acknowledging our own worth and importance, we take the path toward appreciating and believing in ourselves and living out our unique, God-given giftedness.

As you take care of yourself, you will see the rewards in your relationships with the people you care about. A woman who knows who she is will experience less uncertainties, anxieties, and doubts in and about herself. This will allow her to feel less threatened, empty, and tired, and to have more energized, honest, and vulnerable relationships. When we take care of ourselves, our cup overflows with good things to share with others.

Taking care of the self is also fun and pleasurable. Imagine yourself enjoying a warm, scented bubble bath, getting a new haircut, or buying a new body lotion. Picture yourself taking a trip to the beach, having your favorite dish in a nice restaurant, or spending some time in your friend's house away from your kids. Dream big—the sky is the limit. Then *do it*!

Jesus took care of himself. He knew how and when to withdraw to care for his spiritual, emotional, and physical needs. He knew he needed to recharge his energy to fulfill the mission he had received from God. As Christian women, we have also received different missions to fulfill. We are called to be good stewards of body, mind, spirit, and the gifts God has given us. As we take care of ourselves, we stride toward fulfilling our mission as Christian women.

May God grant us the courage to cultivate this lifelong discipline, so we may become the women God created us to be.

Questions for Reflection

1. What does taking care of yourself look like for you?

2. Identify at least two needs in your life which are screaming for personal care. If you cannot identify your needs, think about one or two personal ways in which you can start exploring and recognizing your needs.

3. Identify two or three fears or obstacles that keep you from taking care of yourself or from identifying your needs. Write three or four lines describing each one of these obstacles. Then describe how you might overcome them.

4. List two forms of taking care of yourself which you will be working on in the following month.

5. Choose a partner from your support group who will hold you accountable for your progress in taking care of yourself.

6. Give thanks to God for the chance of making your own choices, for the teachings that come from one's own mistakes, and for every single day which brings new opportunities to enrich your life.

Suggested Resources

Bepko, Claudia and Krestan, Jo-Ann. *Too Good for Her Own Good*. New York: Harper & Row, 1990.

Capacchione, Lucia. *The Well-Being Journal*. North Hollywood: New Castle, 1989.

Louden, Jennifer. *The Woman's Comfort Book*. San Francisco: Harper Collins Publishers, 1992.

Servan-Schreiber, Jean-Louis. *The Art of Time*. Reading, Mass.: Addison-Wesley, 1988.

Woolf, Virginia. *A Room of One's Own*. New York: Harcourt Brace Jovanovich, 1929.

Epilogue

*P*erhaps you have worked hard with this book and the issues addressed within it. Perhaps you wish you had worked harder. Perhaps you're overwhelmed by all the growth that awaits you. Perhaps this book has filled you with more questions than answers. Your response, whatever it is, is fine. Tomorrow is a new day, a new beginning with yourself and God. Tomorrow lies before you, as clean and windswept as a hillside covered with new snow. This book is but a beginning.

Life is a journey—one traveled under the shadow of God's mercy. If this book has raised issues for you, continue to work on them. In doing so, you will open yourself to the life God longs to bring you. Yet be gentle and patient with yourself, trusting God with the speed and depth of your progress. In God's time, all shall be well.

Peace be with you, and blessings upon your journey.

Anne and Nora

Notes

Chapter 2

1. Elisabeth Schüssler Fiorenza. *In Memory of Her* (New York: The Crossroad Publishing Company, 1985), pp. 106-118.

2. These definitions were adapted from *Webster's Encyclopedic Unabridged Dictionary of the English Language* (New York: Portland House, 1989), pp. 1057 and 1184. The definition of sexism was based on the definition of racism.

3. Schüssler-Fiorenza, *In Memory of Her*, pp. 99-101, 118-140.

4. *Ibid*, p. 130.

5. *Ibid*, pp. 118-130.

6. *Ibid*, p. 123.

7. *Ibid*, pp. xviii-xx, 140.

8. Elisabeth Schüssler Fiorenza has identified the movement to recover women's history in the Bible as "Hermeneutics of Remembrance." See her book *Bread Not Stone* (Boston: Beacon Press, 1984), pp. 19-20.

Chapter 3

1. C. S. Song, *Theology from the Womb of Asia* (New York: Orbis Books, 1986), p. 63.

2. Rosemary Radford Ruether, *Sexism and God Talk* (Boston: Beacon Press, 1983), p. 23.

3. Elizabeth A. Johnson, "The Incomprehensibility of God and the Image of God Male and Female," *Theological Studies* 45 (September 1984), p. 441.

4. *Ibid*, pp. 455-456.

Chapter 4

1. Anne Wilson Schaef. *Co-Dependence: Misunderstood—Mistreated* (San Francisco: Harper & Row, 1986), p. 39.

Chapter 5

1. Mary Field Belenky, et al. *Women's Ways of Knowing: The Development of Self, Voice and Mind* (New York: Basic Books, Inc., 1986), p. 6.

2. *Ibid*, p. 8.

3. *Ibid*, p. 152.

Chapter 6

1. Adapted from the work of John Bradshaw, *The Family* (Deerfield Beach, Florida: Health Communications, Inc., 1988), and from the poetry of Marilee Zdenek, *Splinters in My Pride* (Waco, Texas: Word Books, 1979).

Chapter 7

1. Linda Tschirhart Sanford and Mary Ellen Donovan, *Women and Self-Esteem: Understanding and Improving the Way We Think and Feel About Ourselves* (New York: Penguin Books, 1985), p. xiii.

2. *Ibid*, pp. 3-20.

3. *Ibid*, pp. 289-290.

Chapter 9

1. Leonard Swidler, *Women in Judaism: The Status of Women in Formative Judaism*. (Metuchen, N.J.: The Scarecrow Press, Inc., 1976), p. 80.

2. *Ibid.,* pp. 83-113.

3. Elizabeth O'Connor, *The Eighth Day of Creation* (Waco, Tex.: Word Books, 1971).

Chapter 10

1. Marilyn Mason, "Intimacy" (Hazeldon Foundation, 1986).

2. I'm indebted to Marilyn Mason for identifying these areas for work, though I've developed my own set of descriptions for each of them.

Chapter 12

1. Joel D. Block, *Friendship* (New York: MacMillan Publishing Co., Inc., 1980), p. 31. Response of a twenty-eight-year-old male to a survey taken to reveal male views of female friendships.

2. Carol Gilligan, *In a Different Voice* (Cambridge: Harvard University Press, 1982).

3. Luise Eichenbaum and Susie Orbach, *Between Women* (New York: Viking Penguin Inc., 1988), p. 15.

4. *Ibid,* p. 23.

5. *Ibid,* p. 22.

Chapter 13

1. The content of this conversation was transcribed by Helen Havlik, and was put in the form of this essay by Nora O. Lozano-Díaz.

Anne Baxter   *Nora O. Lozano-Díaz*

Contributors

*T*he editors and writers of this material are five women bonded by a great commitment to deal with women's issues from a Christian perspective. They met each other during 1986-1991 at Eastern Baptist Theological Seminary (Wynnewood, Pa.). All of them have been involved in support groups, whether as members or leaders. All believe in the power that emerges from telling one's own story and struggling with one's own issues.

Editor *Anne Baxter*, an ordained Presbyterian minister, is associate pastor of the Union Church of Manila, Philippines, (an interdenominational, international, English-speaking congregation).

Anne was born in Columbus, Ohio, in 1964 but spent most of her youth with her two sisters and parents amidst the stone houses and farmlands of Bucks County, Pa.

In 1986 Anne received from Wheaton College a B.A. in social sciences. Her degree focused on the HNGR Program (Human Needs and Global Resources). To fulfill program requirements, Anne completed a seven-month internship in the Philippines, under the direction of the Institute for the Studies of Asian Church and Culture. She lived in a squatter community in Quezon City and studied the effect of the local church on the community. She did research and writing for ISACC regarding a variety of social problems facing the Philippines.

After college graduation, Anne returned to Pennsylvania and worked as historical researcher, studying the history of old villages and homes in Bucks County. In 1991, Anne felt called to full-time ministry and entered the M.Div. program at Eastern Baptist Theological Seminary in Philadelphia.

During her seminary years, Anne became deeply aware that Christians need spiritual direction to grow in Jesus Christ. Also during seminary she became aware of the many issues facing Christian women and the lack of resources for addressing women's concerns. These factors were what led Anne to her involvement in *Woman's Work*.

During her first year of seminary, Anne became a member of Doylestown Presbyterian Church and shortly after began the process of ordination by the Presbyterian Church, U.S.A. Following seminary graduation, Anne devoted a year to Clinical Pastoral Education at Thomas Jefferson University Hospital (Philadelphia) and a year to unordained ministry at Grace Presbyterian Church (Jenkintown, Pa.). On November 6, 1993, she was ordained and three days later began her ministry in Manila.

Editor *Nora O. Lozano-Díaz*, Mexican born, has been involved in the issues of women in theology and the church as a speaker, writer, pastor, and leader of support groups for women. Her writings have appeared in publications and daily devotionals in both her native country and the United States. In addition, she has been involved in issues of peace and justice in Central America.

She holds a bachelor's degree in social communication from the Regiomontana University in Monterrey, Mexico, and an M.Div. from Eastern Baptist Theological Seminary. She is pursuing a doctoral degree in theological and religious studies at Drew University.

Lozano-Díaz lives in Vincentown, N.J., with her husband, Paul D. Kraus (pastor of the First Baptist Church of Vincentown), and their daughter, Andrea Olivia (1992). She is involved in a support group for young mothers in the Baptist church in Vincentown.

Helen Havlik grew up in Grand Rapids, Mich., and now lives in Unadilla, N.Y., where she is pastor of two Presbyterian churches. She received a B.A. in English from Michigan State University, and an M.Div. from Eastern Baptist Theological Seminary. Prior to seminary, Havlik worked in corporate communications for a Philadelphia-based insurance company.

In addition to her presbytery responsibilities, she serves on the board of directors of the Protestant Campus Ministry in Oneonta, N.Y. Several of her poems have been published.

Elouise Renich Fraser is professor of systematic theology at Eastern Baptist Theological Seminary and a member of Gladwyne (Pa.) Presbyterian Church (USA). She is a graduate of Columbia Bible College, Fuller Seminary, and Vanderbilt University.

Renich Fraser has been writing, speaking, and learning about women's concerns since being a seminary student. She is coauthor (with Louis A. Kilgore) of *Making Friends with the Bible*, Herald Press, 1994.

Her husband, David A. Fraser, teaches sociology and biblical studies at Eastern College (St. Davids, Pa.). They are the proud and grateful parents of two adult children, Scott and Sherry.

Carol Young Schreck is assistant professor of marriage and family ministries at Eastern Baptist Theological Seminary and a marriage and family therapist in private practice at the Kairos Counseling Center in Paoli, Pa. She and her husband, Peter, professor of pastoral counseling at the same seminary, often teach and counsel together.

Schreck is a clinical member and approved supervisor with the American Association for Marriage and Family Therapy. She holds degrees from Houghton College as well as from Azusa Pacific University, where she earned an M.A. in marriage, family, and child counseling. Prior to pursuing graduate studies, she taught in the public school system in Buffalo, N.Y., and Boston, Mass.

Born in Hamilton, Ont., she is an avid sports enthusiast. She and Peter enjoy skiing, tennis, and swimming. They have two adult children, Jonathan and Rachel.